Blessings of the Burden

Blessings of the Burden

Reflections and Lessons in Helping the Homeless

ALAN R. BURT

WILLIAM B. EERDMANS PUBLISHING COMPANY
Grand Rapids, Michigan / Cambridge, U.K.

WM. B. EERDMANS PUBLISHING CO.
2140 Oak Industrial Drive N.E., Grand Rapids, Michigan 49505 /
P.O. Box 163, Cambridge CB3 9PU U.K.

Printed in the United States of America

19 18 17 16 15 14 13   7 6 5 4 3 2 1

Library of Congress Cataloging-in-Publication Data

Burt, Alan R., 1953-
Blessings of the burden: reflections and lessons in helping
the homeless / Alan R. Burt.
pages   cm
Includes bibliographical references.
ISBN 978-0-8028-6860-2 (pbk.: alk. paper)
1. Church work with the homeless.   I. Title.

BV4456.B87   2013
261.8´32592 — dc23

2013001750

www.eerdmans.com

I
dedicate
this book to
my wife, Dawn,
whose faith in me
and whose love for me
sustains and strengthens me
in my struggles for the homeless

CONTENTS

INTRODUCTION

I begin this book with a prayer:

> Dear Creator, I thank you for the opportunity to follow your will by loving and helping the poor, the ill, the oppressed, the homeless. I trust that you have guided me in the writing of this book, and that I have said what needs to be said. I pray that you will use what I have written to open the minds and hearts of readers, that they may lend a hand where it is badly needed. I am deeply grateful for your presence in my life, and that you continue to bless me with all that I need. Amen.

To paraphrase and adapt a quote from Martin Luther King Jr.: "There will be generations of regret regarding how poorly the homeless have been treated by some, and the appalling silence of the many."

I say that now is the time for us, the many, to speak out for those most in need, to demand that our local, state, and federal governments honor the words of our Pledge of Allegiance: "One nation under God, with liberty and justice *for all.*"

In what follows I am speaking out.

I began my work with the homeless in 1993, and by 2001 it had become my life's mission. Over the years many people have referred to me as one of the biggest advocates for the homeless they have ever known. I appreciate the compliment, but the truth is that there are many others who have done much more. In fact, I am already thinking of writing a book about these amazing people, these heroes in our midst.

My self-determined role and function has been to provide the homeless with a voice, to be a voice crying out to the wider community for their needs and rights. My voice has been loud and at times irritating to the many who feel that the homeless are undeserving, or are simply not their problem. I have been quick to criticize those who hold these prejudiced and oppressive attitudes. In this role as an advocate for the homeless, I have spoken in churches, in town halls, to the press, on the radio, and even on my own public television program, *Hearts for the Homeless*. I have been a voice for those without a voice, and it has been a privilege, an honor, and a blessing to speak out for them.

In the pages that follow, you will read about Henry, a seventy-seven-year-old homeless man whom I came to love and respect deeply. Shortly after Henry's death I felt his presence behind me; he was whispering, "Hey, Al, write a book about the homeless. Let the people know about us. They'll listen to you. I know they will." Even as I write these words I can feel Henry's spirit again, smiling behind me, reminding me of his presence, his love for me, and his gentle insistence that I write this book.

Let me give you an overview of the book you are about to read. In Chapter 1, I write about several of the homeless men and women I have come to know and love. You will see that although I helped them, I feel that they have helped me even more. By this I mean that each of them changed me in such a way that I became a better human being. My hope is that this book will help you to experience the blessings that I and others have found in coming to know, love, and help the homeless — blessings that I suspect some of you may already have experienced. "Truly I tell you," Jesus said, "just as you did it to one of the least of these who are members of my family, you did it to me" (Matthew 25:40).

In Chapter 2, I introduce you to Billy Bishop, a man who lived on the streets for ten years. Through my conversation with Billy, you will learn what a lost sheep thinks, feels, and does while wandering the wilderness of the streets. You will hear his profound contention that we people of faith need to wake up and step up to help our brothers and sisters in need. Thousands are suffering and dying on our streets while most of us sit back in our comfort zones, as if we had no responsibility to help make things right. As Billy once said to me, "Is it really enough to merely pray for those in need?"

In Chapter 3, I offer an overview of the "perfect storm" of factors contributing to the homelessness crisis in America.

In Chapter 4, I discuss the struggles my own community had in dealing with homelessness, and how our struggles reflect those of all communities.

Finally, in Chapter 5 I introduce an innovative and cost-effective approach in addressing the problem of homelessness in America.

I conclude with some closing thoughts and supplemental materials, including a photo gallery and some information about Homeless Not Hopeless, Inc., an organization you will read more about in the pages to come.

My Christian faith will be evident throughout this book, but I hope that I have written broadly enough to encompass the beliefs and philosophies of all who endorse the notion that loving and caring for those most in need is our responsibility as good neighbors. I believe deeply that a Higher Power, by whatever name we choose to use, appreciates all the many words and ways we use to better comprehend our lives' meaning and purpose, which ultimately boils down to the extraordinary, beautiful calling to love and help one another.

In the silent worship of the Quaker faith, to which I belong, the limitations of words and concepts are lessened as we sit in silence to communicate with the Divine and with each other. In a similar way, I reach out to you, my readers, to help me write this book. As I think these thoughts, I can feel your presence inspiring me. We are not alone. We are interconnected in ways seen and unseen. Let us therefore reach out to those most in need to let them know of our love and support of them.

CHAPTER 1

My Journey to God through the Homeless

F OR AS LONG AS I can remember I've heard about the poor, the sick, the oppressed, the homeless, and how it is our responsibility to love and help them. At the same time, though, an inner voice has always raised a challenge: *Why should I bother with "those people"? Am I my brother's (or sister's) keeper?* Yet like Cain in Genesis 4, I have had to confront the implications of this question — as I believe we all do. Ironically, the very people I tried so hard to avoid for so long have become the most important people in my life.

In this chapter I will share the stories of some of the homeless men and women I have come to know and love. (To protect their confidentiality, I will not use their real names.) I will try to convey my great gratitude for coming to know, love, and help them. I will share how these experiences have led me to important reflections and lessons about living life. I will share how these men and women changed me, blessed me, and transformed me into a better human being. Although it's true that I helped them, I sincerely believe that they helped me more.

As you read these stories, I ask that you reflect on those times in your life when you helped someone in need. What reflections did you have, what lessons did you learn, what blessed you and helped you become a better human being? How wondrous and mysterious that in helping those most in need we come closer to God! Truly this is why we are here, our meaning and purpose on earth.

BIG TOM

I can't remember when I first learned that the homeless were "good-for-nothing bums," but I know it was early. I remember once when I was just six or seven years old. I was playing alone in my front yard when suddenly I saw *him* about twenty feet away. Big Tom was walking down the road; he passed by me while I stood paralyzed in fear, convinced that he was going to kill me. After all, he was a very bad man — at least so I had heard. Some of the kids said he had been a mobster; there were rumors that he had killed people. Some people said he was on the run from the FBI, CIA, or maybe from the mob itself. They said he had been very wealthy, that he used to drive around in a Cadillac, but that he had lost everything. Now he was old, the town drunk, living in a shed in the woods. I breathed a sigh of relief that he walked by as if I wasn't there.

A few years later I had a very different kind of experience with Big Tom. Again I was playing in the front yard, this time with my brothers. To our shock and fear Big Tom came walking up our driveway. We ran to the back yard, yelling, "He's going to kill us! He's going to kill us!" How surprised we were when my grandmother came to the door and welcomed Big Tom in with a smile. We tried to listen outside the door to what they were talking about, but we couldn't hear much. It was obvious that Big Tom was crying and that my grandparents were trying to comfort him. And then I heard Big Tom say, "No, I can't take your money; you don't have it to spare." My grandfather said, "Today I do have it to spare, and it's yours." I heard Big Tom stand up, so again I ran away. For a long time I forgot about this experience, but in the back of my mind it stayed with me.

Years later I thought of Big Tom as I sat and listened to a man talk about how we don't listen to God, even though God speaks to each of us every day. I don't remember the man's name, but he told me that the reason we don't come to know and love the poor is *because God wants us to know and love them.* I was confused; I asked what he meant by that. He said, "We are self-centered and self-serving in so many ways and on so many levels. The idea of reaching out to those in need challenges our core beliefs, like the belief that everyone is responsible for himself or herself, that I am not my brother's or sister's keeper. We therefore deliberately choose not to listen to the things God asks of us and continue serving ourselves instead." I was surprised: "That's a rather cynical notion about us, isn't it?" He replied, "Sadly so."

The more I thought about it, the more I realized he was right. Like so many others, I spent most of my time focusing almost exclusively on my own needs while so many around me suffered. Was I defying my Creator's will? Was I really so self-absorbed that I wasn't the slightest bit interested in what God wanted of me — to know, to love, and to help those in need?

....

REFLECTION. **I have a vision of a future time, of meeting Big Tom in heaven, of embracing him and letting him know that he began opening up the mind and heart of a young boy, and thanking him for becoming a spiritual guide for me into adulthood. Perhaps this "bum" was in some sense an angel after all.**

7

....

LESSON. We must teach our children not to be afraid of the poor, the sick, the oppressed, and the homeless. Teaching them love, compassion, and commitment to helping will make them strong and wise. To do otherwise only harms them, makes them self-centered and self-serving, and moves them away from God.

....

BLESSING. Although Big Tom could never have known this, my spending just a few moments watching him would one day help to transform my life from one of self-centeredness to one of love and service to those most in need. Just as my grandparents helped him in his time of need, Big Tom blessed me in my time of need as well. Perhaps this was his way of returning the favor. Although it has taken years for me to realize and actualize it, I have been blessed by Big Tom.

....

THE MAN ON THE STREET CORNER

At the age of thirty-five I was pursuing my master's degree in social work at Boston University. One evening as I was walking to the bus station to go home, I passed a homeless man sitting on a curbside. I felt that same fear in the pit of my stomach that I had felt so many years ago when Big Tom walked by me. I decided to follow the drill I had learned somewhere: *Walk by quickly. Don't look at him. Definitely don't talk to him.*

However, as I neared him he looked up at me and with a gentle voice asked, "Could you spare some loose change?" To my dismay, he was talking to me. I was caught, like I had been with Big Tom nearly thirty years earlier. But this was not Big Tom and I was not a little boy. "No, thank you," I muttered as I walked by.

It was about a two-hour ride home from Boston. The whole way I was perplexed and troubled by this interaction. Why did I say, "No, thank you"? There were any number of other things I could have said — so why that? It didn't make sense to me, and I was distressed by it. All through the night I tossed and turned, and early in the morning I realized what had happened. This stranger in the night had asked me, in effect, *if I was interested in helping someone in need.* To that, I had politely said, "No, thank you." I thought about this man and his soft-spoken words all day, his offer for me simply to do something nice.

....

REFLECTION. Why is it that we freeze up when approached by a homeless person asking for spare change? I've talked to enough people to know that this is a common response. Why is it that we're always concluding that they would only use the money for drugs or alcohol, that our helping them would really only hurt them? As I further reflected on my encounter with this man, this stranger sitting on a street corner in Boston, I began to cry, saying to myself, "I pray that if I am ever asked again to help someone in need that I will never say, 'No, thank you.'"

....

LESSON. Throughout the Scriptures we are instructed not to judge others, especially those most in need. We are also instructed to love our neighbor as we love ourselves and as we love our Creator.

....

BLESSING. I believe that this man and Big Tom were angels, sent here to bless me by helping to open my heart to those most in need.

....

Although my interaction with that homeless man on that street corner was a powerful experience, it was not until about five years later that this calling would take me places I never imagined I would go. For example, one day I was driving through the streets of Hyannis, Massachusetts, where I live. I suddenly realized how purposefully I had been avoiding Winter Street. The reason for my avoidance was clear: Winter Street was where the local homeless shelter and Salvation Army were located. It was where *those people* hung out all day and all night. The dirty-looking men and women carrying those garbage bags and pushing stolen shopping carts. Those scary, shadowy figures who frightened me and others. Why did they choose to live that way? Now, contrary to my own reasoning powers, I found myself turning onto Winter Street — and slowly turning into the parking lot of the Salvation Army.

I was terrified as I walked into the building to ask how I could help. Yet in addition to the strange call I felt, I knew I was needed, could do some good. After all, I had a graduate degree in social work. I was invited to begin leading a weekly cognitive change group. When I did, I was surprised by how attentive these homeless men and women were, how engaging their questions, their answers, their insights. In fact, I began to feel that I was learning as much from them — more, even — than they were from me. Again I was perplexed and troubled. What was going on here? What was happening to me?

As the months went by I began to question what I was doing. It was hard to put my finger on it, but I knew that something was happening inside me, something about my attitude and belief systems about the homeless. My old way of thinking about them didn't make sense now that I had come to know so many of them.

First of all, I came to realize that the homeless weren't

the lazy bums I had thought they were. I learned that most of them were very fragile medically, mentally, and physically. They were exhausted. They were desperately in need of housing. *How can anyone get well while being homeless?* I thought. Soon my "think positive, and plan your day accordingly" lessons seemed rather stupid. These people needed love. They needed kindness. They needed housing. I began to feel very inadequate in my efforts to help them cope.

I began talking to other workers to learn more about the issue of homelessness. I learned that there is a housing crisis across the nation, and that homelessness is on the rise. I learned that Section 8 housing vouchers are a very good thing, but that the waiting list was one to three years long. Indeed, by the writing of this book that length had increased to five to ten years. I thought, *How can we, the system, allow people to wait on the street for literal years before helping them into a home? This is wrong, very wrong.*

So, rather than being the useless teacher, I began simply to listen. I listened to their heart-wrenching stories. Most of us take for granted the blessings we have had our entire lives. Although everyone has their share of troubles, most of us have had some loving support to help us through our difficult times. Most of us have been blessed with sound minds and bodies to help us deal with the challenges of life.

Yet not everyone is so fortunate. Some have suffered greater losses, had less support, fewer opportunities to succeed. Some have had to cope with disabling physical and mental illnesses, making it all but impossible to avoid falling to the street, penniless and without help.

....

REFLECTION. **How is it that we think so unlovingly about such men and women?**

How is it that we simply leave them to suffer and die?

....

LESSON. Clearly we should not scorn and judge those who fall to the streets. Our Creator wants us to love and help our neighbors in need. Like lifeguards, who simply pull people out of the water because they have fallen into the water, we should be pulling people out of homelessness because they have fallen into homelessness.

....

BLESSING. Although enlightened to the plight of the homeless, I was about to have an experience which would dramatically change my life forever. This transformation began with an encounter I will now share.

....

GLEN

Glen was one of the first homeless people I came to know and truly love. He was a strong advocate for the homeless and was often banned from the neighborhood shelter for his sharp tongue and bold behavior. Glen had joined the alternative church shelter group that Rev. Bob Huff and I started through the Hyannis Salvation Army. Glen loved spending the nights in the churches, and he was well loved by many of the church volunteers.

Years earlier Glen had managed a motel in town. He said he had convinced the owner to lower the rates in winter to make rooms affordable to the homeless. He used the logic that a little money each night was better than no money at all. Glen's life was going well until the night he came home and found his wife dead from a heart attack. He was devastated, and eventually drank himself to the streets. After losing his home and his car, Glen fell hopelessly into homelessness.

Glen used to apologize for being so weak, for being so grief-stricken, for becoming so lost without his wife. Yet I told him, "You don't owe me or anyone else an apology for the way you grieved. I've been married twenty-six years and can't say for sure how well I would do if my wife died. It's possible that, like you, my grief would overwhelm and disable me."

In significant ways Glen helped me to empathize with the homeless. In one way or another, each of their lives had fallen apart. Though one could argue that they could have or should have handled their losses and difficulties differently, who are we to judge? Perhaps one day we will face a challenge too overwhelming as well! Who will be there to understand our pain, our needs, our dysfunction? Will we be rejected and left to die on the streets?

In 2003, a law was passed in Massachusetts prohibiting public health insurance funds from being used to extend coverage beyond a three-day detox hospitalization stay. If a long-term rehabilitation bed was not available upon completion of the detox, insurance coverage ended and a homeless person would be returned to the streets. When one of Glen's friends died, he came to me and said, "My dearest friend died in the woods like an animal — like an animal!" He said this loss was too much for him, that he had relapsed and was afraid of dying. He got himself into detox, but because of the new law he was unable to stay. "Alan, I'm not going to make it. I'm not going to make it," he told me. A couple of days later, while I was attending the memorial service for his friend, Glen died in a motel room.

Glen's death remains one of the most difficult ones I have ever faced. I admired and loved him. I benefited greatly from our conversations; I learned much about life from him.

Through all his troubles, he never lost his faith in God, and he never stopped helping others the best he could.

....

REFLECTION. I've often wondered how well I would be able to handle the troubles and tragedies that Glen and so many others have endured. Would I become all the more self-centered, worrying only about my own situation, or would I be like Glen and become a loving support and a resource for my peers?

....

LESSON. No one believes it could happen to them. The nearly 700 homeless men and women I have met didn't believe it could happen to them. Yet they found themselves on the street.

....

BLESSING. In his life and his death, Glen blessed me by introducing me to the hearts and souls of the homeless. As I have come to know many homeless men and women, I have become a better person of faith and a better human being. In important ways I have Glen to thank for this.

....

SARA

I had known Sara for a long time. She was one of the unfortunate ones who seemed destined to die on the streets because of her alcoholism and failing health. One morning, after I spent the night with some of the homeless, I noticed her walking across the parking lot toward the door. I was tired and eager to leave. I wondered what she wanted from me. I thought seriously about hiding — not because I was afraid, but because I was irritated.

Yet it was too late; she saw me. Did she want something to eat? Did she just need to use the restroom in the shelter? As she approached the door, I opened it. "Hi, Sara. What can I do for you?" She looked at me for what seemed like forever and finally said, "May I come in?" *Oh, no,* I thought. *This is going to take a lot longer than just making a sandwich or two.*

I asked again what she wanted, but for some reason she seemed to need to build up to her request. Impatient, I remarked that I had just been on my way out the door and asked her again what she needed. She apologized with such sincerity that I was touched. I concluded that she had been drinking. I tried to be patient, but I began to feel uncomfortable as she moved closer to me as if she wanted to whisper something into my ear. She gazed into my eyes, and in a very soft voice asked, "Will you pray for me?"

Here I had been waiting for her to ask for food, for a ride, for something, and all she had wanted was for me to pray for her. I was speechless. She asked me again, "Will you pray for me?" Blessed and honored, I prayed for her right then and there. I prayed silently, as we do in my tradition, and we stood quietly for a few moments. Then, with tears streaming down her face, she said, "I'm not well. I have a heart condition and I'm going to die soon. I don't want to die like this, Alan. I don't want to die like this. Please pray out loud for me. I need to hear the words so I know they have been said and have been heard by God. Please, pray for me."

Now tears were streaming down my face, too. I prayed, "Dear Creator, Sara and I are gathered here in your name. We are reaching out to you, reaching out for your love and kindness. Sara is in real trouble; she is frightened for her life, and so in need. Please help her, God. Help her find the safety, the peace of mind, the help and support she needs to

15

be in a better place. Please help me to love and help Sara. All of this, I ask of you. Amen."

When I finished, we hugged. I said, "Sara, can I give you a ride to the hospital or someplace?" And this time I really meant it. She looked at me kindly and said, "No, thank you. I just wanted you to pray for me." She kissed me on the cheek, said she had to go, and walked out the door.

....

REFLECTION. Ironic how just a few minutes earlier I had been in such a hurry, but now I seemed to have all of eternity to simply watch her walk away. I kept repeating to myself, "I have been blessed by her. I have been blessed by her. I have been blessed by her." These precious thoughts stayed with me for the next few days and then intensified as I learned she had been found dead on one of the sidewalks in town. Not much was said about her death, but I will never forget it.

....

LESSON. The very homeless people whom I used to ignore, judge, even detest have become the most important people in my life. I was blind and now I see. I was lost and now am found.

....

BLESSING. Sara came to me, asked me to pray for her. Because of this, I have been blessed by her. Sara, more than anyone else, helped me to understand what Jesus meant when he said, "Truly I tell you, just as you did it to one of the least of these who are members of my family, you did it to me" (Matthew 25:40).

....

This encounter and the prayer I said for Sara had a profound, enduring effect on my life. Suddenly it was crystal clear that I was on a journey to God through the homeless. I had heard the call of Matthew 25, and I had responded. I could have learned this lesson many years earlier, but I chose to evade it, believing it would require too much of me. It was simply too important to know, so I hid it from myself all these years. In such a simple and profound way, Sara helped me to understand the love and hopes God has for me, for all of us.

HENRY

Henry was a close friend of Glen; he died in my church shelter program. Henry and Glen were quite a pair, always trying to outdo each other with the stories they told. Henry had a knack for coming out on top, which annoyed Glen to no end. Like Glen, Henry was a smart man. He had earned a bachelor's degree and was an engineer earlier in his life. He was always talking about his wife, who had come down with Alzheimer's disease thirteen years ago and had been shut away in a nursing home. Henry eventually became so brokenhearted that, like Glen, he fell to the streets, a seventy-seven year-old man sleeping behind dumpsters at night.

I don't think I've ever known a man more gentle and friendly than Henry. Everyone loved him; everyone felt awful about his wife. Like Glen, Henry had helped the homeless when he was younger, going out at night to look for people who were intoxicated on the street and bring them home. Now, though, he was an alcoholic and not in good health.

I had several conversations about Henry with shelter staff, who were concerned that other homeless people were taking advantage of him. They said that he was handing out hundred-dollar bills when he got his SSI checks at the beginning of each month. When the staff asked him about it, he would snap, "I have more money than them, and it is my choice to help those less fortunate." I wonder how many of us would be handing out hundred dollar bills if we were homeless.

Henry used to joke about being a boxer in his youth. "I had one hundred fights and won all but ninety-nine of them. I won the fight when my opponent didn't show up," he would say. "My knuckles would get so swollen that they had to stop most of my fights. Yeah, the referees kept stepping on them."

Along with his wonderful sense of humor, there was a real wisdom about him too. You might remember it was Henry whom I had a vision of behind me saying, "Hey, Alan, write a book about us." I remember one night, listening to him talk to a couple of people while he was reading an article about Hurricane Katrina. Henry said, "It's wonderful how we are helping these people, but I wonder how long it will be before *these people* become *those people.*" Henry was right; before long, newspaper stories began to reflect an attitude change about the victims, a feeling that "they" were taking advantage of "us."

When Henry died, a doctor at Cape Cod Hospital asked who this man was, since so many people had come up to coronary care to visit him. "He was so loved by so many," she remarked after he passed. She was right; Henry was greatly loved and would be greatly missed.

....

REFLECTION. More than anyone else, Henry has reminded me of my grandfather, who died when I was eleven. I lived with him, and in some ways never got over his loss. Like my grandfather, Henry had a gentle way about him, a warm sense of humor, a wisdom that always left me wanting more. I truly miss him.

....

LESSON. We have been taught to think of the homeless as different from us. In truth, they are just like us, but desperately in need of our love. When we understand this and do the right thing in helping them, something happens, something mysterious, wondrous. We come to more deeply know and love God.

....

BLESSING. I cannot help but smile whenever I think of Henry. He was a sweet old man who blessed me with his love, his life. As with my grandfather, I remember special times we had together, things that Henry said to me that I will never forget. I was too young to be at my grandfather's side when he died, but was with Henry when he passed on. I have been so very blessed in knowing and loving Henry.

....

ETHAN

Ethan was a young man, very tall, very attractive, who suffered greatly from drug addiction. I was saddened when I learned of his death on the streets, but my sadness was not from knowing him, but from not knowing him. I had only a few interactions with him, but one of them is destined to stay with me forever. I walked over to the shelter one night and Ethan was there and asked if he could go to one of the churches for the night. I dreaded the question, as I had promised the churches that I would only send those who were clean, sober, and safe to be in the program. Because I had too many concerns about Ethan I said, "I don't feel you're ready for this program." I was touched by his humble response. He put his head down and simply said, "I understand."

....

REFLECTION. As I walked away, I pondered his response. Years have passed, yet I still remember it so well. I can visualize our conversation as though it had just happened.

....

LESSON. In my brief relationship with Ethan I learned to not be afraid of those who were most lost. Although I could not reach them, could not help them, I could greet them, acknowledge them, which in itself is so very important. Ethan helped me to learn the lesson that sometimes just a smile and a hello can start to bring someone back from the hell he or she is living in.

....

BLESSING. For a time I felt haunted by Ethan's death, but I came to feel blessed by it — blessed by Ethan, who helped me to really understand some of the most important things: worthiness, forgiveness, and compassion. Ethan helped me to better understand and feel the love and mercy of God.

....

HANK

One morning after spending a night with some homeless men in a church, I was packing up the linens and mattresses and taking them downstairs to the van. After carrying a bundle downstairs, I came up and saw Hank standing at the top of the stairs. I expected he was there to help me. But as I picked up another bundle, I noticed that he had not moved. As I came back up the stairs and saw him again, just standing there, I thought about how ungrateful he was. I avoided eye contact with him this time and carried another bundle downstairs. As I came back up, Hank said, "Hey, Al, can I help?" I said, "I'd really appreciate it." But after carrying down one bundle, he again stopped at the top of the stairway. After I carried another bundle or two down, he said, "Hey Al, can I carry another bundle?" I said, "Sure," and pondered what had just happened.

REFLECTION. **After being on the streets for a time, so many homeless people become so deeply depressed that they are deadened to themselves and the world — so low in self-esteem, self-worth, that they do not feel worthy to participate in the world. It is enough for them to simply exist each day. In this saddened state they are like young children who need to be watched over and taken care of, as they are no longer able to care for themselves. Now I understood why so many of the homeless don't seem interested in getting better. Many of them no longer have the vision that their lives can get better, so they think,** *Why try anymore?*

LESSON. **Rather than judging and condemning the homeless, our role as people of faith is to find the lost sheep and to bring them back to safety.**

BLESSING. **Hank in his time of weakness and dysfunction helped me to understand the meaning of mercy, kindness, and unconditional love. Although I continue to struggle with my tendency to believe that people need to be more responsible, Hank helped me to develop the patience to wait for this without an attitude. In this, I have become a better human being.**

MITCH

Mitch was a college graduate, a smart man who once hoped to become an attorney. The deepening effects of depression would prevent Mitch from attaining this life goal. Yet unlike most, who would have become bitter from these events and from being homeless, Mitch found a special place at the local Salvation Army. He was one of those amazing volunteers who did everything from cooking to cleaning up to watching the door. I came to know Mitch from his volunteer role as doorkeeper.

I've thought about Mitch often over the years. He was a kind and generous soul. He had a magnetic smile. When Mitch smiled at you, you had to smile back; it was impossible not to. At certain times the Salvation Army doors were locked, but Mitch would sit inside and open the door when someone approached. Then he would greet you with that wonderful smile. Even if the person coming in wasn't able to get what he or she was hoping for, there was always that wonderful reward, that blessing they would get from him at the door.

Mitch died while crossing a road to get to his camp in the woods. The newspaper article said, "A man was killed crossing a street. No charges will be filed." Now, if this had been a person with a home, a job, the driver would have been charged. But homeless people don't count for much. At least Mitch died on the street where he lived. That might not mean much to many, but it means a lot to me.

Months later I was talking to a woman who lived near where Mitch was hit by the car. She mentioned a night in which a man was hit and killed. I interrupted and learned that it was Mitch. She said, "I held him in my arms and told him he was loved and I cried uncontrollably as he died in my arms."

....

REFLECTION. I thought to myself how blessed they both were in those last moments of his life. How sad the world was not paying attention, did not know Mitch, did not love Mitch, did not care about Mitch's death.

....

LESSON. When I think of Mitch I am reminded that it is so easy to focus on the weaknesses of the homeless. However, if you take the time to listen to them, to really get to know them, you find that they are remarkable human beings in the midst of great suffering.

....

BLESSING. Mitch was a shining example of a kind and loving man. I will always remember his smile, and how in greeting you he would make you feel like the most important person on earth. Perhaps we should all honor each other this way.

....

BIG JOHN

When I think of Big John, I think of the phrase, "Appearances can be deceiving." Big John was well over six feet tall. With his height, a large scar on his face, and a scraggly beard, he did have a menacing appearance. "I'd hate to meet him in some dark alley" is what lots of people might say about him. If I hadn't known him, I would certainly have said the same thing. But I did know him, and the truth is that if you were in danger in some dark alley, Big John is someone you would hope would be there too, as he would lay his life down for you in a heartbeat.

Often I would see Big John on the couch in the shelter, just sitting there. I once asked him about this. He said, "I can't stand the thought that my being here might mean that someone else doesn't get in, so I sit here and when I hear the worker say, 'We're full,' I get up and say, 'No you aren't,' and leave." Big John would rather have slept outside than take someone's bed. And on one cold and blustery winter night, outside is where he died. I have been told that people went out that night and tried to convince him to come in, but he said he was calling it quits, that life was simply too long and too hard for him to accept any longer.

....

REFLECTION. This tall and menacing-looking homeless man broke a lot of hearts with his passing. I find it mystical that, one year earlier, Big John was the best man at a wedding of a homeless couple that took place on the very spot where he froze to death.

....

LESSON. Big John was a remarkable, memorable man. From the way he passed, I learned a valuable lesson about helping the homeless. You can't rescue them all. Some of them are going to die in this war. Yet we must not despair in this, but rather become strong from it, so that we can continue to do what we can to help those who can be saved. The alternative is burnout.

....

BLESSING. I was blessed by Big John from our few interactions. He once thanked me — not for anything I did for him, but for what I was doing for others. His acknowledgment meant a lot. It came out of nowhere, as if he had been watching me from a distance and then giving his report.

....

JAMES

I was blessed to know James for nearly two years. He was one of those elderly people with an amazing memory of days long past and the ability to tell fascinating stories. He told me how his family could not afford to feed him during the Depression, so they turned him over to the state and he ended up with a family who really only needed another laborer to make ends meet. As soon as he was old enough, he enlisted with the Armed Forces, serving in World War II and Korea. Afterwards he worked various jobs — including one as a watchmaker. He had a unique ability to make these stories come to life. We especially loved to listen to his stories about being a soldier, as it was so clear that he was very proud of his service. Often he would wrap up his war stories with a phrase that became his trademark: "Imagine that!"

James told us how he had volunteered to drive some soldiers home after the war and how a number of families no longer wanted them, as they had changed too much, didn't fit in anymore. "Imagine that!" He recalled the big push in the 1970s to move the mentally ill out of locked mental institutions. This was not about helping those people, James said, it was about saving tax dollars. There was no place for many of them to go, except the streets. Nobody wanted them in their town and nobody wanted to help them anywhere else, either. "Imagine that!" Ironically, James ended up homeless himself during the last ten years of his life.

One day he looked into my eyes and said, "Why am I still here? There's no place for me now. I can't afford the rent; it's too high. There's no point in my living." In so many ways, his plight was the same as that of our soldiers, our mentally ill, our homeless, and our elderly in this country. Once your youth and your contributions to society are used up, you'd better be financially stable or you're in danger of being tossed to the streets to die, like James and so many others.

James died just one month after we found a home for him. After his death, the police found his niece. She said that she had been looking for him for ten years. She said that he had been living in a veterans' housing facility but had been moved three times because of a lack of funding.

One day, he packed his bags and announced that there didn't seem to be enough funds to help him. He walked out the door and went on to live on the streets for the last decade of his life. He said, "I'm a soldier. I can take care of myself."

His niece said that James was a wonderful human being who had treated her like a princess during her youth. She went on to say how heartbroken she had been when he hit the streets and how grateful she was to us for having come to know, love, and help her Uncle James.

....

REFLECTION. **James was a soldier in two wars. Even in his eighties and homeless on the streets, he was independent and proud, a soldier to the end. How is it that we forget about our heroes, leave them to suffer and die on the streets of America?**

....

LESSON. **James helped me to become painfully aware of the plight of our elderly veterans as more and more of them are falling to the streets, left to die. As James would say, "Imagine that!"**

....

BLESSING. **I felt honored that James showed up and allowed me to help him into the churches each night, that this soldier felt at home with us, felt safe with us. And so many of us enjoyed listening to his stories. We were all blessed by James in so many ways. Imagine that!**

....

BRENDA

Of all the homeless men and women I have known, Brenda is one of the few whom I have worried about the most. She suf-

26

fers from schizophrenia and depression and not surprisingly is isolated. She spends most of her days wandering the streets. Sometimes she shows up at the shelter for a bed. Sometimes she does not feel safe there and sleeps outside. One cold winter night Brenda came to the door of the church where I was sleeping with a group of homeless men. She asked if she could come in. I was happy to see her and welcomed her in. Over the years I had often wanted to help her, but she would always politely decline and move along. But tonight she was safe and warm, and I felt blessed to have her with us.

When it was time for bed, I realized that she had not taken off her coat and was still sitting in a chair. I approached her and suggested that she lie down and go to sleep. She stared blankly and did not answer me. I went off to my sleeping area, questioning my ability to reach people like Brenda and trying to figure out how I could improve myself. I tossed and turned the whole night long, feeling as though I had failed in some way.

In the early morning, Brenda got up and began to exit the building. I happened to be standing in the hallway where she would need to pass. When I saw her, I felt the same sense of failure and loss. I had not been able to comfort her, to give her a place to rest. I thought of how exhausted she must be, having spent the night in a chair. Although thoughts of her were foremost in my mind, I had no reason to believe that she had any thoughts about me at all. And she had asked me once not to talk to her because it made her nervous when people talk to her, so I remained silent. Yet as she approached me, I silently prayed: "Lord, watch over and protect Brenda, help her to feel safe and blessed." In this moment, I felt this was all that I could do and was about to turn into the kitchen to make breakfast. To my surprise, she stopped and looked into my eyes and said, "You saved my life," and then walked out the door. There are no words to describe how blessed I felt in that moment. Several years have gone by, and Brenda and I have never spoken again. Yet I remember that night and especially that morning when she blessed me.

....

REFLECTION. When I think of Brenda I am reminded that there is so much more taking place than we are aware of. It is so easy to get lost in our senses of what is going on that we forget that more than being physical human beings, we are eternal souls as well. For reasons known and unknown we are all here in this physical world to do something together. My faith tells me that we are here to love.

....

LESSON. Brenda taught me to trust that every prayer, every act of love counts — counts more than we can ever know. From her I learned not to question so much and to be more accepting that what I do is enough. This lesson has helped to reduce my anxiety, my stress in this work. If not for this lesson which she taught me, I think I would have burned out years ago. I still worry about Brenda, but I am assured that our Creator is watching over her, watching over all our homeless neighbors, watching over us as well.

....

BLESSING. Brenda helped me to not be afraid of the mentally ill. In fact, she helped me to open my mind and heart to them, as they need acceptance, support, help, and love. In time I would become an advisory board member of the Department of Mental Health. Brenda helped me onto this path.

....

JANIS

Janis was a very bright woman who had achieved considerable success in the world. Yet with the late onset of schizophrenia, she had lost her job and her place in her family and world. She ended up driving her car to Cape Cod, where it broke down and she began her days on the streets. She was the stranger in town whom I had had the good fortune to meet and bring into the care of the churches. A deeply religious woman, Janis loved going to the churches, the synagogues, and the Quaker meeting house and talking with people of faith.

One of the things I cherished about Janis was the way she greeted me and everyone else. She spoke with such great enthusiasm, seemed so joyful to see us and talk with us. The sound of her voice saying your name made you feel like the most important person on earth — and as soon as someone else came along, she would do the same for them. I always looked forward to seeing her and hearing her call my name.

One day Janis was beaten up and robbed on the street. Although visibly shaken, she was happy to be alive and grateful to be among friends. That enthusiasm in her voice was still there. As soon as I learned that she had lost her suitcase, I emailed my list of church volunteers to see if anyone had a suitcase they could spare.

That evening Andy and his wife Martha drove down to the parking lot where we were waiting for the church cars to pick the women up for the night. Andy had volunteered a couple of times when the women stayed at his church, so he knew who Janis was but really didn't know her well.

As soon as the car stopped and Andy stepped out, Janis was running across the parking lot, calling, "Andy, Andy!" When she reached him she gave him a big hug and said, "Andy, so good to see you." Now Andy had only spoken to her a couple of times, so he was very surprised that she even remembered him, let alone knew his name. He was so taken by surprise that as he exclaimed, "You know who I am?"

tears rolled down his face. Yet Janis exclaimed, "Of course I know who you are, Andy. Of course I know who you are!" They hugged as if they had known each other forever.

I can put this story into words, but there is more than just the events that happened. During the moments that passed here it was if I was in a future time and in another place. Somehow I knew this was a reflection of my own experience meeting the Creator at the end of my life. I had died and had approached the gates of heaven. I had not yet spoken to anyone and was feeling unworthy being there. I looked off into the distance and saw our Creator talking with several others. I thought to myself, *I am not worthy to be here,* and began to turn away. Yet in this moment of despair, the Creator ran over and embraced me and exclaimed, "Alan, Alan, it's so good to see you!" Shocked and amazed and with tears flowing down my cheeks, I exclaimed, "You know who I am?" "Of course I do, Alan, of course I do."

REFLECTION. I call this "the suitcase story," but while Janis got the suitcase, Andy and I got something much more precious, so precious that it is hard to explain. We had a vision of that time and place where each of us will get that first glimpse of our Creator, who will know us and greet us in the most personal and loving way.

LESSON. Janis helped me realize the incredible importance of the homeless in my life. In the beginning I thought I was the helper. Over time I have come to realize that perhaps I have been helped the most.

BLESSING. Janis blessed me with the vision of a future for all of us. She also blessed me with her enthusiasm and love for everyone. She was with us only a little

while longer, and then one day disappeared without notice. I never saw her again, but I have never forgotten her.

....

CONCLUSION

In this chapter I shared brief stories about a few of the homeless men and women I have come to know and love. I have not provided case studies or analyses; I have only shared moments I had with each of them. It is my prayer that these stories have enlightened and inspired you to the amazing possibilities for becoming involved or more involved with the homeless. My fellow workers have confirmed how even the most brief moments with a homeless person can be so meaningful, so spiritual, so life-changing. In these instances we are transported to other places, to other dimensions of experience too mysterious and unfathomable to talk or write about. Mother Teresa explains this well when she says, "In the face of the poor, the sick, the homeless we see the distressed disguise of God." All I really know is that each of the men and women I wrote about brought me closer to God. It has been my great joy to share these stories, these treasures, with you.

CHAPTER 2

An Interview with Billy Bishop

MORE THAN ANYONE ELSE, Billy Bishop has taught me about the homeless — who they are, what they need from those of us who aren't homeless, and what they can do for themselves. Billy is president of Homeless Not Hopeless, Inc., an organization founded by and for the homeless. The organization houses, supports, and advocates for the homeless in the Cape Cod community; you will learn more about it later in this book. In this chapter I share an interview with Billy in which we talk about homelessness and the issues that surround it.

Good morning, Billy.

It is a good morning isn't it, Alan? It sure is.

Tell us a little about yourself, please.

I'm president of Homeless Not Hopeless, Inc., an organization created by and for the homeless for the purpose of providing supportive housing, resources, advocacy, and most importantly love. I am a voice for the homeless.

What about your qualifications?

Well, I lived on the streets for ten years, so I'll say I've earned a doctoral degree in homelessness. It may seem like I'm trying to be funny, but I'm not. You can't get to know what I know by taking courses and adding degrees to your name. What I know comes from real experiences and from the heart, the best of times and the worst of times, if you know what I mean.

What am I talking about? I'm talking about sleeping on the ground night after night for years. I'm talking about seeing things and feeling things that I can only pray most people will never know, like finding a dear friend frozen dead to a tree and having to walk away in fear that somehow you will be blamed for his death.

Can you imagine how it feels to be making an anonymous phone call to the police to say there's a dead man near the railroad tracks and then watching from a distance as the police and rescue respond? It's an experience that really cannot be put into words. I find myself emotional, hurting again, just talking about this. Alan, I have seen things, felt things, done things that no one should ever have to see, feel, or do. That's really all I can say about this for now.

Can you say more about what the homeless think and feel?

Well, I can tell you what they think and feel in the sense that I've been there and I've known and loved many others who have been there too. Too many of them are dead, but I still remember them, will never forget them. In fact, they are a big reason why I'm here today talking with you — to make a difference. I was pulled out of the gutter, brought back to life for a reason. I'm on a mission now. I used to be a fisherman. I caught fish for a living. Now, I'm a fisher of

the lost sheep: our brothers and sisters in need. My job is
to find those who are lost and get them into my net of love
and kindness. Don't ask me how I do it, but I can bring
them back. I've counted 126 homeless deaths in the past
twenty years, right here on Cape Cod. So many of these
deaths could have been avoided if there had been enough
help available. My God, we've got people out here. It is
time for us to wake up and step up.

Look, Alan, I'm embarrassed to even talk like this. I'm
sounding like I'm a holy man. In truth, I'm nobody, I'm
nothing, and I really mean this. All I can tell you is that
our Creator wants me to do this work, and I'm going to
do my best. I nearly destroyed my life, and I was brought
back through the love and kindness of others. I am so very
grateful, and I owe so much, so very much.

Now, I'm not saying that I'm expected to do this. I've
chosen to do this out of free will, out of gratitude. Each
time I bring someone back from near death, I am reminded
of my own gratitude for having been saved. How I wish
everyone could feel what I feel when I make contact with
a lost sheep, and how through my own experience, having
been a hopeless wretch myself, can say words that reach
them, that bring them back, bring them back.

*Billy, I remember hearing your name come up in a lot of meetings
in the 1990s, when we felt you weren't going to make it through
another winter. For many, you were considered beyond help, hopelessly addicted to alcohol and destined to die on the streets with
others like you.*

That's exactly right, Alan. I had lost all hope of ever becoming well again. I had given up. I had learned from my

own experience and from the experiences of many others that sometimes life gets overwhelming and we have breakdowns. Oftentimes these emotional breakdowns are not crushing blows. You slip in and out of a sense of doom as you have the support system you needed to help you through it. Other breakdowns are more severe, leading a person to a period of dysfunctional behavior which further complicates his or her problems. But again, with supports and resources, a troubled life comes back together again.

I think most of us have experienced periods of depression and dysfunction in our lives. But some get knocked down so hard at times that they simply can't get up, or will not get up, unless someone lends a hand, a hand up. Well, when you're homeless, have nothing but the clothes on your back, feeling rejected and hated by the community, it's not hard to feel like life simply isn't worth living anymore. Once someone really gives up he or she begins a death march which takes many forms: addiction, depression, dysfunction, death.

Billy, one of the most frequent things I hear is that everyone is responsible for themselves. Do you agree with this?

Alan, I would have to say yes and no. Yes, the alcoholic or addict has to want to become sober again and has to take each of the steps to get there. No one can do this for him, or for her. But there's more to it than this. We as individuals and the community need to assume some responsibility for finding and rescuing those who are lost and at risk of harm. We can't simply leave them out there to suffer and die.

It's so easy — and I say irresponsible — for us to simply sit back and say that the homeless got themselves into this mess, and it's their responsibility to get themselves out of it. It's this kind of thinking that makes deaths on the streets seem so acceptable and justified. It enables us as individuals and as a community to feel no responsibility whatsoever for any of this. This is so wrong, so very wrong.

The question I keep asking the community is this. Are we our brothers' and sisters' keepers? Whenever I ask this, there is always an awkward silence. I say the silence comes from the feeling of discomfort in really knowing the answer and knowing that we have not shown the compassion, the love, and the help to those most in need. We go to worship each week to pray and praise our Creator, promising to be more spiritual and loving, and all the while people are suffering and dying on our streets with little to no help from us. There's something amiss here, something awfully amiss.

Alan, you've talked about Glen, how finding his wife dead in their home was simply too much for him to handle. He slipped into depression and dysfunction and died in the process. You've also talked about Henry, and how his wife getting Alzheimer's disease was simply too much for him to handle, how he ended up on the streets because of this as well. Like Glen and Henry and many of our homeless neighbors, I have a similar story. I had the best parents in the world. I was blessed, absolutely blessed. My childhood, my life couldn't have been better. I had everything I ever needed and more. I was loved and cared for, had a life filled with blessings.

Like many people, I drank too much. As I look back at it now, I was a functioning alcoholic for most of my life. There are millions of functional alcoholics. I would now argue that no one should drink at all, but that's another long story. As an adult, I was a fisherman for nearly forty years.

I loved fishing, truly loved it. It was difficult for my father
to understand and accept this. For years he tried to get me
to take over his business instead. In fact, this did cause a
bit of a rift between us. But we still loved each other dearly,
and I do mean dearly.

My father retired and one day came fishing with me. He
showed up the next day and the next day and the next day.
He ended up working for me on my boat for nine years. I
remember one day when I knew he had something important to say to me. He said, "Billy, now I understand why you
love to fish. I love to fish, too. I love to fish with you." Now,
I have to tell you, there is no amount of money, no treasure
great enough, to come close to the importance of hearing
those words from my father. We fished together for nine
years, and the bond we made with each other was incredible.

My mother was the sweetest human being you can
imagine. She was always there for me, always loving me,
guiding me in the most precious ways. Again, I had the
best parents and family in the world. But my father died
suddenly of a heart attack, and my mother died eleven days
later. I was crushed, totally crushed by this. My alcoholism
deepened its grip on me. I was no longer functional. I fell
to the streets as a hopeless drunk. I drank in misery, which
only brought about more misery, to the point where I was
lost to myself and humanity. Now, some might say that I
should have been stronger, that Henry and Glen should
have been stronger. Well, as I said before, sometimes people get knocked down in life, like getting knocked out in a
boxing ring. The blows are simply too big, too damaging,
and one needs to be lifted up by the caring, healing arms of
others. If the arms are there, you get picked up. If not, then
you stay there and die.

Now, I'm not trying to blame anyone for my years of being down. All I'm trying to say is that I was down, and it was going to take a real effort, a real, long effort from people truly committed to lifting me up from the darkness and back into the light, into life again. I was saved through the love and kindness of people of faith.

Tell me more about being lifted up into the light.

I was saved by you, and others like you, who never gave up on me, never stopped trying to help me. All too often what happens is that people try to help someone but only to a point — then they give up. Well, when you give up on someone who isn't going to find the strength to pick himself or herself back up, that person will continue to suffer and might even die. We have a responsibility to do all we can to help those most in need, no matter how difficult they make this work for us. Even then, some will give up and die. What's important is that we do our best to love and help those in need. Because of funding problems, there are too few workers out there to do this important work. Sadly, this lack of time and resources is, in my opinion, causing people's deaths. I was clearly destined to die, but I was saved by the love and efforts of people like you, Alan.

I owe each of you everything, and I vow to spend the rest of my life paying it forward. When I began to do this, I found myself increasingly blessed. *How can this be?* I used to think to myself. I thought that dedicating my life to helping the homeless would be hard work that would require great sacrifice and heartache from me. Instead, I find myself feeling so filled with joy and peace each day that I serve my brothers and sisters in need. I was blind; now I see.

I'm not alone in this joy and blessing. I see this miracle of rebirth and transformation happening all around me. I see other drunks and addicts coming back to life as I came back to life. They are becoming an army of angels here on earth to help others out of the darkness and into the light. Some of us have a defined religion and use this as our guide. Others are simply doing the work that needs to be done for love's sake. All of us are filled with great love, joy, and peace as we are helping those most in need.

I was the lost sheep that the Scriptures talked about, and I can tell you about my misery, my guilt, my shame, my depression, my wish to no longer exist. In my view, I had disappointed my parents by ruining my life, choosing alcohol over everything else. I had become a worthless bum, a vagabond. I created this hell, and I lived in it. Living on the streets as a drunk was what I deserved. I was dead to myself and the world. Many people tried to help me out of this hell, but I simply didn't care anymore. All I wanted to do was drink myself to death, plain and simple.

I was warned again and again that if I continued on my path of self-destruction that I would die on the streets. I was told that my liver would explode or I would be found frozen to death on some cold winter morning. People meant well by trying to scare me. But in truth, I wasn't afraid of death. I was afraid of having to live another day feeling the way I did. I despised myself and my life. I waited for it to be over and vowed to drink myself to death as a monument to my misery on earth. I was no longer a man. I was an animal, unworthy of anything but misery and death. And this is how I thought, how I felt, how I lived my life for ten years on the streets.

Now, others would argue here that I was a caring friend

to a number of people, that even in this hell I was doing good works. As I look back, some of this is true. However, none of it mattered. I was lost in my misery, disgusted with my life through and through. I drank to escape my misery and to find death — and the sooner the better. Let me tell you about one of my nights, which might help you to have a closer look at the way I thought and felt, the way I existed.

It was early evening and near freezing outside. I was tired and hungry and disgusted with my life. As I walked slowly out of town, I thought to myself, *I'm no longer a man. I'm an animal looking for shelter for the night.* Tears came into my eyes as I thought about my life as a child, when I was loved and part of a family, a part of the human race. But I was a man no more as I turned into the woods for a place to sleep for the night. *Even a dog has a doghouse,* I thought to myself. *I have nothing, I deserve nothing. I despise and hate myself. Although I'm tired, it is so cold and I'm shivering. I need to drink more so that I can simply pass out. This is the only way I'll sleep. If I'm lucky I won't wake up. If I'm lucky this is my final destination. It is time to be no more, to be no more.*

I was nearly asleep now, not restful sleep, but passing out sleep. I'd drunk enough to kill the pain, enough to make me think I was not freezing to death. I could feel the icy cold on my face but somehow it didn't feel cold anymore as my mind shut down for the night. I knew my body was in trouble, near death trouble, but it felt so good, simply slipping away, my mind slipping away, no thoughts, no worries, no cares, simply slipping away. This was what I looked for in the bottle, not to feel good but to be able to pass out, to slip away at the end of another day in hell. *With any luck,* I thought, *I won't wake up and will simply be no more.*

Life can be cruel, and it was cruel again for me as I did

wake up early in the morning. As I slowly and painfully arose I could hear the crackle of the ice on my chest. I was near frozen to death and shivering wildly. I was in a panic for survival. I knew I had to start walking, to find somewhere indoors to warm up before it was too late. It always came down to this.

Although I wanted to die, I was a coward and each time I came close to death, I went for help. It was the survival instinct, and it kept me alive for years on the street. This is what I mean by not being human anymore, as the human part of me clearly wanted to die. But the animal part of me by instinct kept me alive. I arrived at the Salvation Army and got myself a nice warm cup of coffee. I was safe again — but safe from what? I succeeded in being able to experience another day of misery. It was sort of a joke. I had the chance to escape this hell by death, which I had prayed for, and blew it. I was still alive — why?

So another day begins for this lost sheep. Someone approaches me and says, "Hi, Billy." I say, "Hi" back, and we begin to talk. I'm not as miserable as I feel, since I do care about my homeless friends, as they are lost sheep too. Lost-together brothers and sisters of the street. We're going nowhere together, which is at least something.

The Salvation Army closes down for the day, and we take a walk down Main Street in Hyannis to get some cigarettes. As we walk into the general store, we get the stare which says, "What are you doing here? You better have money on you." However, no words are spoken, which is good, which means we are allowed to stay and conduct some business. But we had better be quick as he may change his mind. Although we may be able to purchase a pack of cigarettes, we are still vagabonds and bums to him.

It looks like I'm going to make it through another day. I don't know what the purpose of this is anymore, but it is time for me to think about where I'm going to sleep. I tried to get into the shelter but they were filled by the time I got there. So I need to go back into the woods again. Maybe I'll take a walk down to the railroad cars and sleep there tonight.

Billy, that sounds like a horrible night. When was that?

Alan, it was many nights. They were all like this, human by day, animal by night. There's nothing more I can say at this time. Thank you for listening to me.

....

REFLECTION. **Billy Bishop has seen and known things we all need to know and see. And, as Billy says, "We need to wake up and step up." It is time to love.**

....

LESSON. **If we are to really understand how best to help the homeless, we need to seek out those among them who can be leaders — who are already leaders. As we acknowledge them, as I did Billy, we not only lift them up, we learn so many important things about the homeless and how best to help them to help themselves and each other.**

....

BLESSING. **I have been blessed by Billy. He has shown me that the hearts of the homeless are beautiful, fragile things, things worth loving and caring for, priceless treasures that open the mind, the heart, the soul. We can find God in the homeless.**

....

CHAPTER 3

The Perfect Storm

I N ANOTHER OF OUR conversations, Billy Bishop described homelessness as the "perfect storm." The phrase intrigued me, and I want to use it in this chapter as I lay out the forces causing homelessness in America today. In what you are about to read, I will not be referring to studies or statistics; many other helpful books and articles offer those. Rather, I will speak simply and personally about the basic elements creating and perpetuating this national disaster. Much of what I have to say will probably be familiar to you already. My intention is to lay it out in a concise and personal way, as I believe we must make the issue of homelessness personal. In fact, I contend that our collective tendency not to personalize and respond to this tragedy is the most significant component of this perfect storm.

The premise that the homeless are victims of a perfect storm stands in sharp contrast to the more popular contention that the homeless are lazy, irresponsible, and hence undeserving of our help. What follows are fourteen of the most significant elements of this storm, gleaned from my own experience and from conversations with Billy Bishop and others. At the end of my discussion of each element, I offer a "Prayer from the Heart," which I invite you to pray with me whether you are reading this book alone or as part of a group.

OUR NEGLECT OF THE MENTALLY ILL

During the 1970s there was a massive exodus from the state mental hospitals. Although proponents argued that the mentally ill had a right to live outside locked facilities, most of us knew that closing the doors of their public hospitals would save states millions of dollars each year. As a result of these closings, many of the mentally ill fell to the streets of America, where they remained. Although some programs were begun to provide services and housing for the mentally ill, their funding was inadequate from the start and has only diminished over the years. It is no mystery why our streets are filled with the mentally ill. We have no place for them, and they have no place to go.

Perhaps more than any other aspect of the homeless, the appearance and behavior of some of the mentally ill is what catches our attention and provokes our fear and outrage. The mentally ill are often the most ragged-looking and publicly offensive homeless people. Yet I argue against the notion that they are the most dangerous. Although many consider them frightening, in truth, we terrify them. They do not understand our seeming hatred of them. With their limited faculties, they respond to our not loving them either with withdrawal and isolation or with anger and outbursts.

So lost in illness, many of them will not ask for help or be receptive towards it if offered. I have learned in my work that they respond best to love and kindness. Yes, they can be loved back to health and wellness. I've witnessed this happen again and again. Men and women whom most people believed could not live independently are living independently with the love and support of good neighbors who have recognized their needs and have been moved to help them accordingly.

I believe that our tendency to ignore or dislike the mentally ill comes from our fear of them. We don't understand them; we feel uncomfortable with them. They are not like us. I used to feel this way about them.

A few years ago I attended a training session that helped me to understand and have compassion for those suffering from schizophrenia, one of the most disabling of the mental illnesses. In one of the training exercises participants were given portable cassette decks with headsets to put on while we walked alone in a mall for twenty minutes. We were instructed to put the tape on once we entered the mall and to leave it on the whole time, even if we had a conversation with someone. In between pauses, the tape featured angry, accusatory voices that made it difficult if not impossible to make sense of the unfamiliar surroundings. After a few minutes, even the pauses were anxiety-provoking, as I began to worry about when the voices would return. At the end of the exercise the other participants and I were more than happy to take our headsets off — which, of course, is something a person suffering from mental illness lacks the option of doing.

I have learned from repeated experience with the mentally ill that if you treat them with patience, kindness, and support they will be very grateful and respond accordingly. Like us, they just want to be accepted, respected, and loved. And of course, when we take the time to extend care and respect to those in need, we feel good inside because we have done something important, something very good. As we treat those with illness compassionately, we become better human beings.

Individually, we are all at different places in terms of understanding and dealing with the mentally ill. Some of us are afraid of them, and either avoid getting involved or do so only reluctantly. Others of us are able to respond to them in caring, even loving ways, and do what we can to help. Still others feel especially called to focus on issues relating to mental illness, but lack sufficient numbers to effect changes at community, state, and national levels. Our pleas for funding fall on deaf ears, as there is little political will to do more than what has already been done for the mentally ill. In fact, most contend that too much has already been spent on them.

As a member of the advisory board of the Cape Cod and the Islands Department of Mental Health, I can provide a perspective which will help you appreciate how poorly funded DMH is. Our budget is among the easiest for the governor to cut. Sadly, over the last twelve years we've lost over a hundred million dollars in state funds. These are funds meant to help our most vulnerable citizens; without them, they suffer and die.

....

PRAYER FROM THE HEART. **Creator, help me to be more understanding, more loving towards those with mental illness. Help me to develop my empathy, my willingness to truly listen to them as they try to express themselves. All too often, I have walked by quickly as if I didn't have the time to say more than a quick greeting. And even when I do talk with them, there is usually so much more I could have and should have said. Creator, help me and others to be more understanding, more sensitive and responsive to those suffering with mental illness.**

....

In addition, help me to be more understanding and accepting of those who are afraid of or angry at the mentally ill. Help me to learn how to reach them in a way that opens their minds and hearts to the needs of the mentally ill. Creator, help us to reach our local, state, and national leaders to advocate for the funds needed to improve the lives of our most vulnerable and troubled citizens.

....

Our Neglect of Those with
Physical Disabilities and Illnesses

I have been astounded by how many of the homeless have serious medical conditions. When we are healthy we take our health for granted. In truth, we are all at risk. Illnesses and accidents do not discriminate. One elderly homeless man told me he sold his house to pay a hospital bill. So many others have told of accidents or medical problems that left them unable to work, and so unable to pay the mortgage or the rent. Eventually they found themselves homeless.

....

PRAYER FROM THE HEART. **Creator, please help us as individuals and communities to be more sensitive and attentive to those with medical and physical problems. It is not enough for us to merely feel sorry for their afflictions. We must take the time to help them with their day-to-day needs. Let us become a community that watches over and protects our neighbors in need.**

....

Our Neglect of Veterans

I am nearly sixty years old, and ever since I was a child I have heard about how our nation continues to neglect the needs of our veterans. Millions of men and women have served our country; many have come home with serious mental and physical problems. While programs have been established to address their special needs, funding and services have never been adequate. Thus, nearly a quarter of the homeless are veterans. While everyone agrees this is no way to treat them, our veterans continue to suffer and die on our streets.

As soon as a person tells me he or she is a veteran, I thank him or her for serving our country, and I listen carefully and respectfully to everything he or she says. It is often difficult for vets to talk about their suffering and trauma. It can likewise be hard for us to listen, as they can tell genuinely troubling stories. I've learned to force myself to pay closer attention to veterans by asking more questions, to demonstrate that I do care and want to know more. Though they tell many different stories, what I hear most is about their loneliness and fear and their need to be heard, respected, loved.

I once sat and listened to a veteran who had suffered long on the streets. He said, "I was once a normal human being. I had hopes and goals like everyone else: marriage, family, work, and play. Then my country needed me so I left home and went to war. I saw sights that no human being should ever see, and I did things that no one should ever have to do. I did not return the same person. My heart was damaged and my mind twisted. I can't sleep. I can't focus on goals. I have no ability to deal with the problems of life. I cry, I yell, and then I'm silent again, and then it goes round and round. Perhaps I'm just crazy now, I don't know."

Another vet said, "I don't feel good about myself and sometimes think it would have been better for me and everyone else if I had just taken a bullet in the head. At least then I would have been respected. Just look at me; I wander the streets aimless and dysfunctional, nowhere to go, nothing to do. Sometimes I'm so angry that I take it out on innocent bystanders who are simply unlucky enough to be near me. At other times, I drink or drug myself into oblivion. As much as possible, I just want to kill the pain and loneliness of my existence. I know I'm not wanted, and I guess I now feel I don't even want to be wanted. I didn't come back from the war. I'm still stuck in the trenches, a living casualty."

Many of our soldiers who are living on the streets have lost their sense of value, purpose, and dignity. It is an honor to acknowledge them, to say thank you. As I continue to do this, I find myself grateful for all the things I have previously taken for granted. As I honor them, I am also expressing my gratitude. In all of this, I am blessed because of them. They stepped forward to protect us. Why is it that we cannot do the same for them?

....

PRAYER FROM THE HEART. **Creator, help our veterans to find the peace, the dignity, and the resources that they so rightfully deserve. I ask that you help us to love and respect our veterans. Individually and as a nation, we need to take care of them. Just as they served us, we must now serve them. Please help us to help them.**

....

Our Neglect of Domestic Violence Victims

Court reports across our nation document the tragedy of domestic violence. Whether it is spousal, child, or elder abuse, the lack of resources currently allocated to properly help the victims is unacceptable. As a result of our unwillingness to provide them with the support and resources they need, too many of them end up on our streets, where their depression and despair turns to dysfunction and sometimes to death.

Many homeless women have been victims of domestic violence. They speak of how they were verbally and physically abused. Many stayed with their abusers, believing they had lost the ability to leave and deal with life on their own.

When some of them did leave, they fell hard to the streets with little to no help. Some retreated back into abusive relationships, feeling they had nowhere else to go. These women and their children are true victims and deserving of our attention, love, and help. Yet all too often on the streets they remain, lost to themselves and to us.

The court systems are filled with domestic violence cases, but experts in the field contend strongly that too little is being done to prevent domestic violence, prosecute offenders, and help victims. Sadly, this ill in our society continues like a plague with no end in sight. As with our veterans, we must pay attention to those who have suffered from the traumatic events of domestic violence. Each time they are listened to and understood it helps them to feel worthy again, helps them to feel that recovery is possible, that they can rebuild themselves and their lives again.

PRAYER FROM THE HEART. **Creator, the victims of domestic violence are often broken down and deeply in need of our time, our attention, our resources, and our love to help them to regain their self-esteem and drive to continue on with their lives. I pray to you, Creator, for your love and guidance, so that the helpers can become more effective in helping our brothers and sisters in need. And I pray for our victims of domestic violence, that they find the strength and ability to recover from the traumas they have endured, as ultimately each of them needs to develop the ability to move forward with their lives. Our love and resources may help them to do this, but the work is theirs to accomplish. May they all find the way to rebuild their lives, to experience all the joys, successes, and peace that each so rightfully deserves.**

And I pray that our leaders become more responsive to this social ill, this crime. Not

only are millions directly affected by domestic violence, but this problem comes at a huge financial cost to us all. This problem is a national crisis, and it must end. As a society, we must not tolerate this lack of attention and response any longer. Our courts need more power and control regarding prosecution of these crimes. Our departments of social services, elder services, and other organizations that provide support and resources need adequate funding to respond to the needs of the victims of domestic violence. In order to accomplish this, we need more effective laws, adequate funding, and programs to more personally and competently address domestic violence.

....

Our Neglectful Response to the Housing Crisis

Since it began in 2006, the housing crisis in the United States has left millions of families homeless. We tend to think of this crisis as a national problem, requiring action on the federal level, but the fact is that local communities have a responsibility to do what they can to help provide affordable housing to families. In my state of Massachusetts, a law was passed in the late 1960s that effectively required 10% of all new housing in every town to be affordable to low-income families. For over forty years, nearly every town in Massachusetts has violated this state law. Yet there have been no violation notices, no penalties. Although providing affordable housing was at one time sufficiently considered a responsibility of our communities to become a state law, subsequent generations have neither obeyed nor enforced this law. Indeed, not only have our communities refused to develop and provide affordable housing, a number of towns have actually developed ordinances which make it difficult if not impossible for homeowners or landlords to provide affordable housing. Landlords in some communities are being given local violation notices for their practice of providing affordable housing — and as a direct result, families are ending up on the street.

Tired, hurt, lonely, angry, and hopeless, those who have lost their homes through foreclosure or eviction become depressed, dysfunctional, and often they simply give up. How does a child develop into a positive and productive adult without a safe, warm, stable home to grow up in? How do men and women pull themselves out of homelessness? How do the elderly, with their decreasing funds and dwindling health, avoid falling to the streets, or worse yet survive homelessness once it has occurred? The housing crisis is about all these questions.

I have come across many individuals who have recently lost their housing. Some of them live out of cars filled with their remaining belongings. Some have furniture in storage with hopes that they will find housing again. Yet many remain in homelessness far longer than they expect. As one woman said to me, "I never thought that I would become one of those people, but here I am, one of those people. I can see the disdain in the faces of storekeepers when I walk in with my garbage bag of clothes. I am looked down upon and despised. They don't really know who I am, who I was, and they don't want to know me. I simply don't matter to them. I have become one of those people. I know now, for sure, I'll end up a drunk or an addict or, if I'm lucky, dead."

....

PRAYER FROM THE HEART. **Creator, these are hard economic times. Millions of men, women, and children are at risk of or are experiencing homelessness because of the housing crisis. Please help us to reach the minds and hearts of our communities, of our leaders, to join hands to help our brothers and sisters in need.**

Our Lack of Sensitivity
to the Jobs Crisis

Along with the housing crisis, the United States has been experiencing an economic crisis for the past several years. There simply aren't enough jobs. As a result, unemployment and underemployment have grown to epidemic proportions. Millions of men and women are unable to make a living wage. Many in America are now living in fear of losing their jobs. And for those who have lost their jobs, even temporary homelessness makes it even more difficult to find work. How do you look your best when you aren't well-rested, when you've had to live out of a garbage bag for weeks? And finding a job is one thing, but being able to keep it is another thing altogether. In addition to not having transportation, the work schedule itself is often problematic. If you stay at a shelter and work during the day, you may not get into the shelter at night because it may be full by the time you get out of work.

For those who do manage being homeless and working, being able to save up enough for first and last month's rent can take weeks if not months. In my years working with the homeless I've watched so many go from being hopeful when their job interviews went well to hopeless when even working doesn't seem to do any good. It doesn't take long to simply give up.

....

PRAYER FROM THE HEART. **Creator, these are desperate times. Please watch over the millions who are in fear of losing their jobs, the millions who have lost their jobs, and the millions who are now living on the streets. They are losing hope, losing faith, and some are even losing their lives. Help them to be strong and help us to**

become less absorbed in our own lives and more involved in their lives. Help us to help those in need.

....

Our Lack of Political Will

Our public officials on the federal, state, and local levels are painfully aware of the lack of resources available to help those most in need. Yet many are hesitant to support requests for additional funding for the poor, as they fear it is an imprudent political move. It takes real courage for politicians to advocate strongly for those in need, as the poor have little voting power and siding with them is both unpopular and unwise in terms of getting reelected. How sad that we live in a world where it is unwise to help the poor, the sick, the homeless!

Yet the homeless desperately need the support of our political leaders. Housing experts have clearly proven that there are less expensive ways to house the homeless than continuing to use the shelter model. During the past few years there has been a lot of praise for housing-first models and rapid rehousing programs which use state funds to help homeless men and women into rentals. Although this sounds like — and indeed is — a wonderful thing, the funds are insufficient to maintain this program, and so the shelter model remains in place. Sadly, the general public lacks sufficient interest in helping the homeless, even if doing so would cost the state less money. As a result, there is a lack of political will to do the right (and cost-effective) thing. The mere discussion of it has become a politically risky thing to do.

OUR OPPRESSION OF MINORITIES

Persons of color and persons from certain places of origin have been oppressed and discriminated against since the very beginning of this nation. Beginning in the colonial period and continuing well into the twentieth century, white settlers took Native American land, oppressing and nearly wiping out the Native American nations. Although generations have passed, Native Americans continue to be among the poorest in our country. Euroamericans likewise oppressed African Americans through slavery and other forms of institutionalized racism. Today, African Americans are statistically poorer than Euroamericans. Until this changes, how can any of us say in good conscience that ours is "one nation under God, indivisible, with liberty and justice for all"?

Neglect of Our Elders

Our elderly population, too, is more at risk of poverty and homelessness than ever before; I have worked with a number of homeless men and women in their seventies and eighties. Sometimes they are victims of the housing crisis and the poor economy, like many people younger than they are. Often what happens is that the death of one spouse makes it impossible for the surviving spouse to afford the mortgage or the rent. Now that members of the huge Baby Boom generation are turning sixty, the number of elderly Americans falling to the streets is not likely to go down. These elders are our parents, our grandparents, our aunts and uncles. How will we treat them in their need?

....

PRAYER FROM THE HEART. **Creator, help us to be more loving and helpful to our elders, many of whom are living in fear of losing their homes. Let us become a nation that truly respects, loves, and takes care of its elders.**

....

Our Discrimination against the Homeless

I remember a conversation I had with a homeless man who was livid after being told he had to leave the public library. "They told me I wasn't using the library correctly! What did they mean by that? I was reading!" Later, I stood by his side when he complained to the town council. Some of the council members said they would look into the matter, but no one ever did.

A while later I read a newspaper article in which a spokesperson for the library openly admitted that the library had a policy limiting homeless persons to spending only two hours there at a time. The article explained that the library had made this rule because of some trouble they had had over the years with some of the homeless. My friend challenged the library board with a letter saying, "If a child acts out, will you then make such a rule for all children? If a black person acts out, will you make a rule for all black people?" He received no response. His concern, and he himself, simply didn't matter.

"All of a sudden I am forced to face the shocking reality that I don't count anymore. I have been hurt, injured by my own community, been neglected and discarded." I have heard countless homeless men and women say things like this when they realize they are no longer considered by most people to be "like us." Over the years, I have tried to become more understanding and attentive to the needs of the homeless. I have made the time to listen to their frustrations, their hurts, their anger, and their resentment for the way they have been treated by the community. Their rights have been violated in many ways. It is commonplace for the homeless to be told to leave stores and other public places. Many towns have taken away public benches so that the homeless can't sit and rest in our presence. Police and others often tell the homeless to move along from our city parks. These and many other incidents of discrimination take place every day; all of them are aimed at making the homeless feel unwelcome and undeserving.

I always feel humbled when I hear the homeless sharing stories with each other of having been discriminated against during the day. It is deeply moving to listen to the support and encouragement they get from their peers, who understand all too well what it's like to be looked down upon by the community. Nevertheless, every community could be doing so much more to help the homeless. It is not a matter of a lack of resources. Instead, it is a matter of unwillingness to end discrimination. If our communities' discrimination were turned into civic responsibility, the problem of homelessness would be greatly reduced — if not eliminated.

....

PRAYER FROM THE HEART. **Creator, help us to be more attentive to the needs and rights of the homeless. Help our communities to prioritize the importance of providing sufficient funds and resources to protect and serve our citizens in need. Let us become strong communities and subsequently a strong nation that truly offers "liberty and justice for all."**

....

Our Abuse of the Homeless

While it could be considered another form of discrimination, I feel that abuse of the homeless is an element itself, as it goes further than just making the homeless feel unwelcome and undeserving. The homeless are often verbally abused, called filthy names by businesspeople, community members, and others. Often the problem behavior of a few of the homeless brings about a negative attitude toward all of the homeless, so that people feel justified in abusing them. Yet what does this say about us as a community, as a nation?

Just as our schools are developing rules against hazing and bullying, so our towns need to develop rules and laws to protect the rights of the homeless, who are also the victims of hazing and violence. As a society, we fail to demonstrate a love for the poor. Until we as a society develop a conscience great enough to love and care for those most in need, the issue of homelessness will continue as the plague of injustice and abuse which hurts us all.

....

PRAYER FROM THE HEART. **Creator, help to soften the hardened hearts of those who seem bent on harming our most vulnerable citizens. Help us to become a more loving community, a community that loves and cares for its neighbors in need.**

....

OUR SELF-CENTEREDNESS

I am bewildered by our capacity as individuals and as a nation to ignore the suffering of others in our midst. The fact is that most of us are aware of this sad situation, yet we continue to do nothing about it. We remain simply too busy attending to our own needs, our own agendas. I know that for most of my life I have been guilty of this very thing. In no way am I pointing fingers. Although I knew there were those in desperate need, I chose to focus on myself, on my own needs and those of my family. It was as if I was saying, "If you aren't a part of my family, or one of my loved ones, you are on your own." It's amazing how easily we can justify our not lending a hand to those most in need.

When it comes down to it we are afraid of the poor, the sick, and the homeless, which is why most of us try to avoid them, avoid thinking about them, avoid doing something for them. We stay away out of fear and justify this fear by agreeing with stories about their being lazy and undeserving. Those of us who have faced this fear still tend to not get very involved. For the same reasons that we don't visit hospice houses and cancer wards, we don't get involved with the homeless. We are afraid that this very tragedy could befall us.

Those of us who nevertheless feel compelled to know, love, and help the homeless do so because we have dared to ask that most personal and spiritual question: "Am I my brother's and my sister's keeper?" For us, the answer has been life-changing. From this inner journey of questioning, we have been awakened to the mysteries of our existence, the meaning of our lives. Here, we have heard God's call for us to love and help those most in need. For those of us who are awakened, we know that there is no greater joy or reward than helping those most in need.

....

PRAYER FROM THE HEART. **Creator, help me to be less concerned and preoccupied with myself and my own needs. Help me to become the kind of person who lives to serve others in need. Help me to better realize and actualize this as the main reason and purpose for my life. Though I may falter from time to time, continue to bring me back to the service of others. Just as I have been served, I want to serve. Just as I have been loved I want to love. Just as I have been saved, I want to save.**

....

Substance Abuse

The stereotypical view of the homeless is that they are all addicts and drunks; if you have made it this far in this book, you will know by now that this is simply not the case. And we should always be mindful that addiction strikes all sectors of society — the rich, the poor, and those in between. Nevertheless, over the past thirty years I have worked with over a thousand men and women suffering from substance abuse and addiction. Some recovered; others lost their battles.

We must all recognize and fear the awesome power of drug and alcohol addiction. Many books have tried to explain how some seem protected from it and how others slowly or quickly become destroyed. We may never figure it all out. From my experience working with the homeless, I can only conclude that using drugs or alcohol is a game of Russian roulette. The only real protection is total abstinence. If you take that first drink, if you try that drug, maybe you will be okay. Then again, maybe you will not be so fortunate.

In addition to the damage done to the self, the collateral damage of addiction is devastating. The need for the drug becomes more important than anything or anyone else. Addiction is the ultimate bad date. It makes people into liars and thieves and destroyers of all that was important in their lives. "I am your enemy," addiction says, "yet I will make you feel like I am your best friend. Like a cat with its prey, I will play with you. I may destroy you slowly, as I enjoy watching you and your loved ones suffer. I may destroy you quickly, as your life bores me. I find it so funny and pleasing that you will probably never fully understand how dangerous I really am and how I really just don't care about you or anyone else. And yet, you keep coming to me to feel better about yourself as if I were a necessary and good thing. My greatest joy is in the pain and destruction I inflict upon your lives. So please, have another drink, take another pill, and let's see what happens next."

Although addiction in and of itself can cause homelessness by making a person unable to work or be a productive member of society, I would also emphasize the lack of funding we have for treating this disease. Unlike cancer and heart disease, whose treatments are extensively covered by most health plans, the limits of a person's insurance policy can mean the difference between life and death. As with few other diseases, addiction allows us to blame the victims. We do this by not providing enough residential programming for them. When I began my work with addicts thirty years ago there were many residential programs that could house and treat addicts for a year or more. Because of funding cuts, many of these programs have disappeared or become 45- or 60-day programs. In a sense, our medical system is telling addicts that they have only so long to recover before they're on their own.

While it may be controversial to say so, I'll finish here by expressing my regret that alcohol is legal. I suspect that this is because, while it clearly destroys the lives of millions, it brings in a pretty profit. The same is true for the overproduction and overprescription of pain medications: they ruin lives, yet they are profitable. It is also true for tobacco products and for so many unhealthy foods. So many lives are at risk in an economy willing to profit from the production and sale of dangerous substances. It is our responsibility as a nation and as communities to provide adequate care for those suffering from the illness, the disease of addiction.

....

PRAYER FROM THE HEART. **Creator, please help us to recognize our need to better care for our brothers and sisters in need. Let us become a nation that does not glorify or glamorize the use of drugs and alcohol. Let us become a nation of communities that provide the support, the housing, and the resources to treat those suffering from addictions.**

THE HURT, ANGER, AND DYSFUNCTION
OF THE HOMELESS

No one ever thinks that he or she could become homeless. Then a series of unfortunate incidents happen and he or she falls to the streets. Suddenly he or she has lost membership in the community and has become one of "those people" who are ignored, talked down to, laughed at, scorned, and told to move along. Filled with hurt, shame, anger, and resentment, some eventually conform to these reduced expectations, this reduced humanity.

The realization that one is unwelcome and hated by the community is hurtful and frightening. Some of the victims of homelessness withdraw relatively quietly into depression and self-destruction through drugs or alcohol. Others express their hurt outwardly through resentments, anger, and rage. Although their thoughts, feelings, and behaviors are inappropriate at times, we cannot say they are not understandable given the tragedy of homelessness. Rather than judge and blame, we should do more to help them.

I remember once being irate with a homeless man. I was coordinating an event to promote National Homeless Persons' Memorial Day, a day which is near and dear to my heart. In addition to holding a press conference and a memorial service, I was preparing to sleep outside on a cold wintry night to demonstrate my willingness to stand beside these men and women. As I was speaking, a homeless man began to yell at me, accusing me of grandstanding, of trying to make myself important, a hero of the poor, while the homeless continued to suffer just as before.

I remember feeling outraged; I even asked a person in authority to make him move along. However, as I lay there in my tent that night, I could not help but think about his resentment, anger, and rage. Although they were displaced, he did have a right to express his feelings. I thought to my-self, *How are the victims of this society supposed to act? Should they be grateful for the scraps given them, and be quiet in their suffering and depression? Or do they have a right to strongly and loudly express themselves?*

I then thought, *Who was I today, to deny him his right to express himself? Perhaps he was right, that I was seeking praise and attention for myself as opposed to really making a difference. Either way, he had a right to express himself.* Suddenly I was confused, no longer confident in my thoughts, words, or deeds. Was he right about me?

Interestingly enough, the next day he walked by as I was taking down my tent. I asked him if he would like the tent, and he readily said that he would, as it was a really nice tent. We talked briefly as we rolled the tent up for him. I then said, "I was angry at you last night for the things you said about me and my colleagues who are simply trying to help the home-less. However, I realized last night as I was freezing in my tent that you had a right to be angry and to express your anger."

He looked at me intently and said, "Thank you; I just wanted to be heard. Just wanted to be heard." We shook hands and he then blessed me by saying that he really did appreciate everything I was doing, that he was just mad. I said, "I understand your anger, as it is my anger too. Home-lessness is a terrible thing, through and through — it is as real as it is needless."

....

PRAYER FROM THE HEART. **Creator, help me to be more sensitive to the emotions of the people living on the streets. They are exhausted, hurt, lonely, afraid, and angry.**

Help me to get to know them, respect them, love them, and help them. I want to ease their pain and sorrow by being the loving arms to hold and help them. Please show me your ways and let them become my ways. Please help me away from my self-centeredness so that I may become more loving, personal, and wise. Please help others to help the homeless, too. As the saying goes, "many hands make light work."

....

CONCLUSION

It is easy to feel overwhelmed by even one of these fourteen elements that contribute to homelessness. How much more so when we look at all of them together and see the perfect storm they create! Sadly, as a nation we have failed to adequately respond to this national disaster. As a result, millions of our citizens have suffered and thousands have died from it.

Throughout this chapter, you may notice that I have strongly emphasized the factor of *us*, the factor of *you and me*. We, the people of this nation, are a significant part of both the problem and the solution. As a collection of individuals we have the numbers and the power to demand that our leaders marshal all necessary resources to help the homeless. Sadly, our leaders are afraid of us, afraid that if they allocated the funds to adequately address homelessness, that we, their constituents, would quickly vote them out of office. As a result, we have become a nation of liberty and justice for some, not all.

How will history record us, the people of a great nation who stood by for so long while so many suffered and died on our streets? Is it possible that we have collectively sealed the fate of millions of our most needy citizens because we were too focused on our own needs, our own selves instead?

CHAPTER 4

Cape Cod's Response

So far in this book I have focused on the *problem* of homelessness — through the many dear friends I introduced you to in Chapter 1, through the wisdom and experiences of Billy Bishop in Chapter 2, and through an overview of the issue's perfect storm of causes in Chapter 3. In this chapter, I want to turn our attention to some unique *responses* to homelessness — particularly those of Cape Cod, where I live. In no way am I attempting to provide a comprehensive picture here of solutions to the problem. Instead, I am simply offering an overview of a series of interrelated initiatives which demonstrate how the homeless themselves have become important leaders in addressing this issue. And in no way am I suggesting that Cape Cod is unique or perfect in its response to homelessness. Every community in the United States has struggled with this complex issue, and ours has certainly faltered in some ways. Nevertheless, we have started to become an effective role model. As Billy has said, "It was time for us to wake up and step up."

COMMUNITY TENSIONS IN THE 1980S

Problems between the homeless and the Hyannis business district began to escalate about thirty years ago. Some would say that the problems worsened with the opening of the town's first shelter. In a conversation I had with Rick Presbrey, executive director of Cape Cod's Housing Assistance Corporation (HAC), he talked about his rationale for opening the NOAH Shelter.

"The word NOAH is an acronym that stands for No Other Alternative Housing. I've been criticized over the years for running this shelter, which has been a headache from the start, partly because of all the money we needed to raise to support it every year.

"What the community forgets, or wants to forget, is that the NOAH Shelter was opened because of the community's failure to provide enough affordable housing. The NOAH Shelter is not the cause of homelessness on Cape Cod. The cause of homelessness is the low-paying jobs and lack of housing that is affordable because costs are driven up by seasonal renters and second-home buyers.

"Over the years we've done our best to get the towns on Cape Cod to provide more affordable housing units. Until this is accomplished, there will be a need for a shelter. As I've said many times, when the Cape increases its affordable housing units for the poor, the NOAH Shelter will lose its purpose, and I will gladly close its doors. However, housing and human service organizations cannot accomplish this without help. The towns of Cape Cod need to do their part to allow more affordable housing to be built and to modify ordinances which increase, not decrease, affordable housing possibilities."

I agree with Rick; it would be ideal to not need a shelter in town. Yet I cannot praise the NOAH Shelter enough, as it has helped so many people and saved so many lives. Let me share one story about the shelter, about the kind of people that Rick has had working there, and you will better understand my praise and gratitude.

One night I walked into the shelter and realized that I had never thanked Tammy, the shelter director, for the loving ways she treated the homeless men and women under her care. I said, "Tammy, I want to thank you for the loving ways you treat the homeless." Tammy responded, "I don't do anything for them." I went on to say, "Come on, Tammy, I'm just trying to give you a compliment." She again said, "I don't do anything for them, nothing at all."

I asked what she meant. She said, "Alan, if I wasn't doing this work I would be so self-centered and self-serving. Here, each of them reminds me of who I am, a child of God. In this, it is they who bless me. Perhaps we have it wrong, thinking that it's us who are helping them. Like Jesus says in Matthew 25, whatever you do for the least among you, it is as though you are doing it to me. Alan, you know what I'm talking about. They are helping us to be nearer and dearer to God." There wasn't much more I could say in response, except to acknowledge that the gift truly is in the giving.

I applaud the work that Rick has done for the homeless. I also agree with him that the opening of a homeless shelter in the downtown area simultaneously helped the homeless and complicated the relationship between IIAC and the community. Yet the NOAH Shelter is hardly the only factor in play. Probably the single most important one is the huge Cape Cod Mall complex, which opened in the 1970s and has expanded continuously since then. The mall took a significant amount of business away from Main Street Hyannis, which had previously been the hub of the Cape.

Nothing could be done about the mall's existence and increasing success; it was here to stay. Yet some in the community began to focus on the perceived negative impact of the homeless on the Main Street businesses. And some became extremely vocal. I remember one public meeting in which a homeless woman stood up in front of a few hundred community members and began to express her shame for being homeless. She spoke about once being a mother and contributing member of society before falling into the depths of homelessness and alcoholism. During a pause when tears were forming in her eyes, one of the leaders in the business community shouted out, "Get a job!" This hateful remark enraged another homeless man, who began walking up and down the aisle, saying, "Here we are in a church trying to find ways, I would think, to love our neighbors in need. Instead, many of you sit here with something else in mind. You don't care about the homeless at all. How dare you come to this church with such evil thoughts and deeds on your minds? How dare you!"

The meeting went downhill from there. Needless to say, some of the homeless did not like these insinuations that they were bad for business and hence unwelcome in our community. Some chose to retaliate by intentionally becoming a nuisance and being bad for business. Hence the battle waged on: "Move along." "Make me." Not all of the town's business leaders adopted this hostility toward our community's homeless; some were and continued to be supportive and loving. Yet the relationship on the whole was complex and troubling.

A COMMUNITY MEETING APPROACH

In the mid-1990s I helped to spearhead a community network meeting to work on the issue of homelessness on Cape Cod. Under the leadership of then-district court judge Joseph Reardon, several important housing, health, and human services leaders began to develop a coordinated community response to the issues of homelessness and mental illness. Several years later this courthouse committee led to the formation of a larger and broader-based committee. In this new group there was more involvement from housing and human services agencies, along with business leaders and public officials.

Nevertheless, in 2002, ostensibly in response to a series of community meetings, a few committee members authorized the bulldozing of the town's homeless camps for "humanitarian" reasons. When the larger committee learned of this, it called an emergency meeting to stop this unauthorized plan of action. Yet it was too late. The more powerful members of the committee had already set the date for their plan to be carried out. Shortly thereafter, the police and the department of public health went into the camps to dismantle them and to put up signs telling the homeless to get out, stay out, or be arrested.

On the day the bulldozers came, nearly twenty homeless men and women were displaced — on the run, frightened, and with no place to go. Rev. Bob Huff, homeless advocate Martha McKeon, and I teamed up to do something to address this crisis in our community. We came up with a plan to rent campsites for the homeless in a nearby state park. It was not an ideal solution, but it was effective and immediate. With a solid plan in mind and our hearts on fire, we joined hands with the homeless. Off we went with them — back to the woods, interestingly enough.

It was in the midst of this crisis situation I had the unique and beautiful opportunity to meet Billy Bishop, to whom I introduced you earlier in this book. Within minutes of meeting him, I felt deeply connected to Billy. He had a twinkle in his eye and was personal and engaging as we talked about the issue of homelessness, the needs of homeless people, and what our community needed to do to help the homeless help themselves.

I spent several evenings in the camp with the homeless men and women. I was deeply touched by their deep sense of gratitude for the space we provided them. Nevertheless, there were many times that summer I questioned the value of what we were doing. We had taken the homeless out of the woods, only to place them back into the woods. It was Billy who helped me realize that something important and extraordinary was achieved here. "These are safe nights, where people can talk and really get to know and be supportive of each other," he said. "Normally the homeless would be staying in small and dysfunctional groups, scattered in the woods, drunk, high, and miserable. Alan, take a look at them now, talking to one another, working together to set up camp each night, preparing the meals, eating together, laughing, sharing their experiences, and giving each other support.

"Alan, just a few days ago they were terrified, and now they are becoming a family. You can't tell me nothing significant is happening here. Something very significant is happening. You, Bob, and Martha have done something very good, very important. I can't explain it all to you. You're the educated ones. I just know, and I think you'll agree when you get a chance to think it all out, that something very important and lasting is taking place here. I'm not sure what the next step is, but I think you will figure that out as well. All I can say is that we are very grateful, and we believe in what you are trying to do for us. As long as you stay by our side, we will be safe and protected. I don't know what else to say."

As Billy spoke to me I was mesmerized by his deep, soulful, unblinking eyes. He was speaking from the heart, and I believed everything he said. It was a spiritual experience. It was also the beginning of an enduring friendship. I have continued to listen attentively to the many lessons he has taught me over the years about the thoughts and feelings of the poor, the sick, and the homeless.

As I look back on that summer at the camp, I can only smile. My wife and I came up with the funds to rent two sites, knowing we needed to be careful not to mention that our campers were homeless men and women who had previously been chased out of the woods of Hyannis. The first evening, I settled into the first campsite with about twenty homeless men and women. I thought the night passed uneventfully, but in the morning a livid park ranger approached me. He said that one of the campers had cut down a small spruce tree to use as a tent post. At first I thought, "What's the big deal, a small tree for a tent post?" Then I learned he had planted this tree himself as a memorial to his best friend, who had died. *The homeless just can't win,* I thought to myself. *Of all the trees in this park, this one homeless person was unlucky enough to choose the one that would get us into so much trouble.* At first he said that we had to leave, but I offered to buy four trees to replace the one that had been cut down. He accepted them, and we were able to stay in the campsites for the remainder of the two-week permit.

In the second state park, we likewise hoped to avoid being noticed. Yet on our second day there, one of the community nurses from Hyannis called me and asked if we had room for a man she had been working with. I picked him up that afternoon. Unfortunately, in the middle of the night he went into alcohol withdrawal, which involved delirium tremens and hallucinations. He cut a hole in the two-hundred-dollar tent I had borrowed and began running up and down the huge campsite yelling, "The Martians are coming! The Martians are coming!" I didn't think the state had as many police cars and rescue vehicles as showed up in response to this outburst.

I remember thinking to myself every day as I drove back and forth from Hyannis to the campsite, *What am I doing, what am I going to do, and what's going to happen to these men and women?* Yet even as I felt overwhelmed and exhausted, I was having the time of my life. I had stumbled into what would be the most extraordinary experience of my life. Little did I know then how spending the summer with the homeless would change my life forever.

The experience changed the campers, too. For instance, I was particularly worried about one woman, Ellen, who seemed very depressed and withdrawn. She usually kept to herself, and in fact I was surprised she had joined us. Yet to my pleasant surprise she became very social and in a short period of time became our cook. Not only did she do a fantastic job of ordering, preparing, and cleaning up, but she also became a camp leader. Various group members would ask to help her, and as they worked together they would begin sharing their problems with her. Right before my eyes her loneliness and despair transformed into confidence and a sense of social purpose.

As Ellen transformed as an individual, our campers transformed as a group. They became a cohesive and productive community. Unlike before, where they were hiding from the authorities deep in the woods, they were now allowed to exist as participating members of a small society. I found myself thinking about the similarities between them and our founding fathers and mothers, who likewise ran from an un-just society where they were neglected and oppressed.

The Power of the People of Faith

I cannot overstate the role that people of faith played in our finding a more caring and competent response to this crisis. Not long after the bulldozing, when things did not look good for the homeless, representatives from over forty churches and other places of worship came forward to advocate for the rights and needs of the homeless. Church leaders and congregation members from all parts of Cape Cod spoke passionately in the town and county halls, to the press, and in public places, insisting that the homeless be treated with kindness and offered the resources they needed. As a direct result of this, our town and county leaders began to listen and respond. Change did not happen overnight, but it did happen.

In fact, within a short period of time, our town and county officials signed a proclamation to address homelessness as one of their most important issues:

And the Assembly of Delegates
Designating December 21,
The 21st Day of December each year
As National Homeless Persons Memorial Day

WHEREAS, the winter poses extreme hardship for inadequately housed, low-income men, women, and children on Cape Cod,

WHEREAS, December 21st has been designated National

Homeless Persons Memorial Day by the National Coalition for the Homeless since 1990 and is so recognized by more than 70 cities throughout the nation,

WHEREAS, the Salvation Army, Cape Cod Council of Churches, Community Action of Cape Cod & the Islands, Duffy Health Center, NOAH Shelter, and other advocates for the homeless planned and convened Cape Cod's first annual event of Homeless Persons Memorial Day on 12/21/03 at St. David's Church in South Yarmouth,

WHEREAS, in this season of generosity and sharing Citizens of Cape Cod are encouraged to commit themselves to promoting compassion and concern for all brothers and sisters, especially those who are poor and homeless,

WHEREAS, in remembering those who have died on the streets, the cause of ending homeless is kept urgent, as is the Citizens of Cape Cod's collective commitment to preventing such deaths in the future, now therefore,

RESOLVED, by the Barnstable County Commissioners and Assembly of Delegates, we hereby declare our recognition of December 21st as Homeless Persons Memorial Day in recognition of the men and women who have died on our streets, in our emergency shelters, in condemned or abandoned properties, from ailments or conditions directly related to homelessness. We hereby declare our commitment to lead the Cape Cod Community in addressing this urgent and moral problem, the plight of the homeless on our Cape Cod Shores.

This document led to an unprecedented amount of town

and county funds being designated to address the homeless problem on Cape Cod. Suddenly, caring for the homeless became a politically right thing to do on Cape Cod. Some elections were won on this very issue.

Many community business leaders, clergy, and other individuals played important roles in opening up the minds and hearts of our community to the needs and rights of the homeless. Royden Richardson, one of our councilors, was one of the first to come on board and advocate for the homeless; councilor Janice Barton was likewise on fire with this issue and became a powerful ally for the homeless advocates and also for the homeless themselves. Through her leadership and connections she got towns from across Cape Cod to donate funds to help the homeless. One project she spearheaded, "In from the Streets," was a program in which homeless men and women could be put up in motels until a better plan could be put into place. She has also slept out in a tent on National Homeless Persons' Memorial Day, which is on December 21 each year. Here on Cape Cod this is a very cold and uncomfortable night. (In fact, I'll never forget the response I got from Janice when I asked her the next morning if she wanted me to get her a cup of coffee. "No, thank you," she said, "I'm sleeping in." As I went off to get coffee for myself and others, I started to laugh: was she sleeping out, sleeping in? Or was she sleeping in, sleeping out?)

Today, the Town of Barnstable and all of Barnstable County has been recognized by the state as having developed and implemented a strong, caring, and competent plan to address homelessness on Cape Cod and the Islands. The work is not done, but clearly under way. In this respect the Cape Cod community has become a model community in addressing homelessness in our nation.

INVOLVING FAITH COMMUNITIES

Faith communities are essential in the effort to help the homeless, on Cape Cod and elsewhere. People of faith are members of congregations who can motivate one another and share resources, and they comprise a large group of voters as well. When ten or twenty congregation representatives show up at a town meeting to address an issue like this, you can be sure that the officials they are speaking to are listening intently.

The partnership between the Hyannis Salvation Army and the Cape Cod Council of Churches has been a powerful collaboration that has brought about many new and effective ways of addressing homelessness on the Cape. Over forty churches and places of worship have served as temporary shelters; huge sums of money have been donated to help meet the needs of the homeless. Through the Overnights of Hospitality program, the homeless men and women in our area became known and loved by many in the faith communities on Cape Cod. As a result, the homeless gained thousands of allies. And not only have the homeless been blessed by the churches; the churches have been blessed by them as well.

As a direct result of the Overnights program, the Council of Churches formed a partnership with the Falmouth Housing Authority in which over a million dollars was raised to build an apartment complex for the homeless. This building, named Bridgeport, has served the homeless well for several years now. In addition to this partnership, the Salvation Army and the Council of Churches have worked closely with a number of other organizations on Cape Cod, including the Housing Assistance Corporation, the Duffy Health Center, Community Action of Cape Cod & Islands, the Nam Vets,

Vinfen, the Department of Mental Health, Cape Cod Hospital, and others.

In addition to these organizational partnerships, many individual men and women have become deeply and importantly involved in helping the homeless. For instance, Dan McCullah, Cindi Glister, and Karen Graveline — a professor, a nurse, and a social worker, respectively — now team up once a week to bring clothes, food, blankets, and supplies to the homeless who live in the woods and are the most lost, most dysfunctional, and most in need. They call this weekly venture "Operation Matthew 25," after Jesus' words in Matthew 25:40: "Truly I tell you, just as you did it to one of the least of these who are members of my family, you did it to me." Through this project they are literally saving lives, and by reading of their example perhaps you, too, will be inspired to do what they do.

Another example of an angel on our streets is that of Izzy Thompson, who has made it her responsibility to meet the homeless at the Salvation Army to write down their needs, whether clothes or personal items. She presents her list to her church congregation, confident that the list will be filled. Lo and behold, the items show up at the church and are then delivered by Izzy to her homeless friends. I have jokingly referred to Izzy as the "Underwear and Socks Lady." In fact, she once got a ten-thousand-dollar grant to buy socks and underwear. Like Dan, Cindi, and Karen, Izzy is a wonderful example how any one of us can choose to become meaningfully involved in the lives of the homeless.

Why do we hesitate? Why don't we respond to the call of Matthew 25? I know that part of the reason I took so long to respond to the call was because of my feelings of shame for not having done so earlier. In truth, it's never too late.

Like Billy Bishop has said, "It's about waking up and stepping up." It is a wonderful moment, a wonderful thing, this waking up and stepping up to the call of Matthew 25. And not only is this the right thing to do for others, it is the right thing to do for ourselves. Truly, the more we do for others, the more we do for ourselves — our journey to God is through those we serve.

One idea for a community to increase public awareness and support for the homeless is to begin holding a memorial service for the homeless each year. The perfect time to do this is on National Homeless Persons' Memorial Day, which is on December 21, the longest night of the year. I organized the first memorial in our community in 2002. Only about twenty people showed up, and most of them were the homeless themselves. We stood in a circle of love while Rev. Bob Huff said a prayer for our friends who had passed that year. Although I was disappointed with the turnout, it was what it was, a beginning.

The next year over a hundred people showed up on the Hyannis Village Green, where a few spoke out for the homeless and the mentally ill. Each year since then, the number of those attending this service has increased. This past year one of the largest churches on Cape Cod, the Hyannis Federated Church, was filled to capacity.

CREATING A NEW TYPE OF SHELTER

As the summer was nearing an end and the state parks were closing down, I talked to Billy about an idea which involved our finding a house for the chronically homeless to live in with staff to watch over them. Billy pointed out that such a program would have to accept these people where they were, which meant understanding that they were not yet ready to become clean and sober. He also cautioned that it would take a lot of love and patience because these homeless individuals were very dysfunctional and subsequently not accustomed to following rules and routines. He further pointed out that most of these people had never succeeded in programs, which would likely make them even less motivated even to try. He said that this would have to be a very different kind of program, one with a very special kind of staff that knew how to reach those who had not been reached before.

I found an abandoned house and asked Roy Richardson, one of the town councilors, to advocate for this program to be developed as a community resource. To say the least, there was strong opposition in the council and in the wider community to the idea of creating yet another shelter. Yet Roy advocated tirelessly for us. Our housing and human services organizations were also developing their ability to advocate and collaborate with one another to make our local and state leaders listen, understand, and respond to the needs and rights of the homeless. And I must again emphasize the very powerful presence of the people of faith who filled the halls with clergy and congregation members who spoke, one after another, on the need for the towns and county to approve of this new shelter for the homeless.

The house, christened the Pilot House, opened its doors about seven months later, its programming implemented jointly by Community Action of Cape Cod & Islands and the Duffy Health Center, two local organizations. At the opening ceremony, Billy Bishop was the first resident to walk through the doors. It was a wonderful sight. He was safe, finally safe from harm, along with several others who were still under the influence of drugs and alcohol. By targeting populations who had been banned or were otherwise not appropriate for the NOAH Shelter, the Pilot House created and maintained a life-saving program for those most at risk of dying on the streets. The Pilot House models how wet shelters can be turned into damp shelters and in time to dry shelters. In a wet shelter, clients are not exprected to remain abstinent from drugs/alcohol. In a damp shelter, clients are expected to be working on their addiction issues. In a dry shelter, clients are expected to remain drug/alcohol free.

ANOTHER LINE FOR BILLY

One evening I met Billy on the street. He was miserable; he had been drinking again. It was clear he had simply given up. A big part of his depression was related to a death of another homeless friend: "Dead on the ground like an animal, Alan, like an animal." Billy took these deaths on the streets hard. "They were my friends. I loved them and they loved me. Now they are dead, dead. Something is terribly wrong here. Laws have been broken."

I felt hopeless. What could I say to him that would be helpful? I remembered his talk about having been a fisherman for nearly forty years. I said, "Billy, you're adrift, going out to sea, feeling like you can never return — and yet there are some of us on the shoreline throwing life lines out to you." He looked at me and said, "Why do you continue to care about me?" I said, "Because I love you." Billy gave me a long, strong hug — the kind that those of us who know him have come to call "a Billy hug."

After our talk, I felt anxious. I was very worried about him. So I called my wife, who said, "You go into the shelter and you bring Billy Bishop home with you. I don't care what it takes, he's out of there. Do you understand me?" So I walked into the shelter and found Billy with his head down. I said, "Billy, I want to take you out of here. Please come home with me right now." With tears in his eyes, Billy said something I will never forget. He said, "I walked in here tonight feeling two feet tall and now I walk out feeling ten feet tall." I felt so happy for him, but did not feel I had done anything special, simply brought someone home for the night. Billy stayed up most of the night talking to my wife.

In the early morning, after Billy had left, I learned he had gotten himself into a program. He has remained sober to this day. Although Billy thanks me for this, I continue to feel what my wife and I did was so minimal, that he was ready to get well and we were simply at the right place at the right time. However, Billy continues to argue this point. "I was lost and you found me through your persistent love for me. What you did is what brings the homeless back to life. Now it's my turn, my turn to find the lost sheep, to bring them back to safety, back to life again. I'll never forget what you and others did for me, and each time I do this for someone else, it is my way of saying thank you, thank you to all of you."

I don't think it's possible to count the number of men and women that Billy has helped over the years. Billy can reach the homeless like no one else. He's been there, to hell and back again. I remember a time when I got a call from an administrator of one of the rehab programs who said that one of the patients had just walked out of the program. She said, "He's very sick, and I think he will die." She asked me if I could talk to Billy Bishop, as she believed he was the only one who could bring this patient back to the program. I called Billy and he said, "I'm on it." Later on that day I got a call that Billy found this man, had a heart-to-heart talk with him, and brought him back to the program.

In the next chapter, I will talk about a new kind of organization, an organization formed by the homeless for the homeless. I'm sure you will agree that this organization has been blessed in so many ways. In truly amazing ways, it has bestowed blessings in return. Not surprisingly, Billy was a cofounder and is currently the president of this organization, Homeless Not Hopeless, Inc.

CHAPTER 5

A New Kind of Organization

I N 2007, I SAT down with four homeless and formerly homeless individuals to discuss something that had
been on my mind for several years, namely, the huge
expense involved in helping the homeless. I wondered if it
were possible to find leaders among the homeless population and provide them some support and guidance to create
their own organization to help their peers. They agreed that
under the current model a huge amount of funding went toward paying administrators and other operational expenses.
They likewise agreed that many of these expenses could be
eliminated if the homeless ran an organization of their own.
As we talked, they generated the idea of a new kind of housing organization: one run not just *for* homeless people, but
by them as well. I told them they were the dream team to
make this vision a reality.

From this amazing conversation Homeless Not Hopeless, Inc., was born. Taking its name from a phrase that a
friend of mine had used to describe himself shortly before
his death in 2003, this new nonprofit's vision was to provide
advocating and housing by the homeless, for the homeless.
With the help of donations from people of faith and the
wider community, within a month we were renting a five-
bedroom home for women and a seven-bedroom home for
men.

I could tell you all about Homeless Not Hopeless, Inc.,

and its work, but I'd rather give this opportunity to its co-founder and current president, Billy Bishop.

Billy, tell me more about Homeless Not Hopeless, Inc.

When a homeless man or woman comes to Homeless Not Hopeless, they are always very touched by our willingness to accept them as they are. Although we have a rule about no alcohol, no drugs, we will weather the storms, the relapses that some of them will have. I mean, what sense is there to make a rule that says, "If you relapse, you are terminated"? Anyone who knows anything about substance abuse knows that relapses happen and should be expected and understood as part of the process. If someone relapses, we talk with them with love and kindness, which is our way of reaching them with what they need to become safe again, safe for themselves and for others in the house.

Instead of threatening them with termination, we talk about loving them and not wanting to lose them. Through this loving interaction, we find a way together to continue on to a better place. We're not perfect in this, but we do the best we can and continue to grow as we move along. Our approach has worked in nearly every situation. The power of love and acceptance is a mighty force. For some, it means going to a detox facility and then a rehab center or long-term program and then returning. For others, it involves a buddy system where they do daily AA for ninety days. For others, the plan involves getting a sponsor and/or entering into substance counseling.

For example, one of our residents, Jeremy, was on his way to a relapse. He announced that he was moving out. We knew he was in trouble and knew that the house he was moving to was filled with people using drugs. We urged him to heed our concerns and begged him to stay with us, where he was loved and was safe. But Jeremy was on the run. He left and within a couple of weeks called me and said, "I'm in trouble." I could tell that he was hoping he could come back to us so I said, "Is it time for you to come home?" He said, "Yes, Billy, I want to come home." I said, "Then come on home."

This is exactly what our HNH houses are about. We take people in and we bring people back. To say a little more about Jeremy, we weathered seven storms, seven relapses with him, before it was clear that we weren't the right program for him. He was gone for over a year and then came back to our door again for help. I had a serious talk with him, gave him a hug and a bed, because that's what we do here. I told him that we would love him enough to watch him very closely and to have additional expectations of him for his own good. Jeremy was grateful and did all that we expected and more, as he knew he was in a safe place with people that loved him and wanted him to succeed. In the two years that followed, he remained sober, attended treatment, and maintained a job.

What we've accomplished with these houses is simply this: everyone is welcome and welcoming. By this I mean that we have a loving culture that promotes safety and well-being for everyone. We talk about this all the time to keep it alive. This culture is like a flower in a flowerpot: so pretty, but helpless to take care of itself. So we water this sacred flower, as we want to continue seeing its beauty. We want to keep this culture of love and kindness alive, so we nurture it every day. We do this by talking about it with each other, sharing our gratitude for living here with each other.

So, unlike most programs, where the house is more staff- and program-driven, our house is community-driven. It is the love and attention of the community that makes the magic, that makes our program work. If someone is in trouble, other community members circle the wagons to offer support, guidance, and resources. If someone is short on rent money, the money is there. If someone needs a ride, the ride is there. If someone is lonely or in trouble, the support and caring heart is there.

My most important role as president is to simply witness the love and kindness that runs rampant through these houses. We are all so blessed here, all so very blessed. I imagine that every program has some similar things to say. What I'm saying different here is that we accept people where they are, which means allowing them to make mistakes and to learn or not learn from them. This is why we don't do drug screens unless we feel it is necessary. We know when it's necessary, as we pay close attention to each resident and know when they are in trouble. If I miss it, then someone else will see it and the community will be alerted to the need to respond with love and care.

This is the magic of the house. We encourage, rather than impose or control. Our role is to love people and guide them — which does get a little confusing at times. Again, we try not to impose and instead to let the resident in trouble know that we care, that we are concerned, that we want to help them the best we can. This approach works nearly every time. I hope this makes sense, as it is a bit difficult to explain. It just works this way.

Has your approach gained any wider recognition?

Who would have ever guessed that a little program like this, with fifteen formerly homeless residents, would get national attention? Yet Phil Mangano, who was appointed by President Bush to lead our nation in a ten-year plan to end homelessness, visited us and wrote about us in his national publication. He spoke about our program having the vision for the future. I have to tell you, I was impressed and grateful for his praise, as it reinforced the value of our work and, more importantly, increased the likelihood for our program and other programs like it to expand.

We need to get away from this over-controlling and over-programming and instead create supportive housing that is more accepting, loving, and tailored to the needs of residents, rather than continue expecting them to conform to our standards. Now, this is the difference between welcoming them to their own home, where they will be cherished and helped, versus warning them to watch their step or else be discharged. I know that many would argue that the latter approach is neater and necessary. However, the former is much sweeter — and, I argue, more successful. I know I can be overly controlling at times, so I watch myself. And yes, I do get reminders at times on this as well. This is a learning experience for us all.

I'm an old salt, a fisherman, and can be a bit much at times, I know. Although I'm working on my gruffness, I'm also aware that sometimes you need to be a little tough on someone who's not getting it and at risk for relapse or other dysfunction. I have seen too many die from this disease, so I know well it is a life-and-death matter. And I've learned that sitting back and watching someone lose their way and not saying or doing anything is not right, not right at all. Just like on my fishing boat there were times of great peril, and as captain I needed to act quickly and demandingly to save the boat and the crew. I'm not trying to make excuses here, just trying to make a point that the gruff, tough-love approach is sometimes necessary. When it is all said and done, I'm a big hugger and my hugs are about love and everyone in my house knows this. And yes, I'm still working on my stuff. Like with everyone else, my stuff is there and I have to deal with it, too. Truly, we are all in the same boat.

How successful has HNH's program been?

Right now we're going on five years of operation. In that time we have worked with over 200 men and women with a success rate of over 85%. By success, we mean that they are either still housed with us or have moved on to permanent housing. We are both a transitional and a permanent housing program. We have a few tenants who will probably never leave, as they need our love, our program, forever. We love them and welcome them here as long as they need us. Most will not need us long-term, and we will help them in every way to move on to the next step when they are ready.

I've got to tell you a little about our board of directors. We have the best board of directors imaginable. We have a retired judge who once sent me to jail; his influence helped us to get the town permit to buy a house to expand our program. We have a high school teacher who has involved his students in raising awareness and raising money. We have a church deacon who has been our spiritual leader from the beginning. Likewise, we have a Quaker business-woman who possesses exception organization and spiritual grounding. We have a man who was homeless himself years ago and is now a financial planner. We have a human services professional and an attorney who both have huge hearts and extensive experience helping people in need. Truly, all kinds of people can be involved in helping the homeless.

And of course we couldn't do it without the help of the many churches and places of worship here on Cape Cod, whose congregations have sent in donations of furniture, clothing, and money over the years. Likewise, the Hyannis Salvation Army has given guidance, food, assistance, love, and support. So many other nonprofit organizations have helped as well. They were there for us, believed in us from the very start. Just as we wanted to succeed, so did every one of these organizations want us to succeed. Without their love and support, we would not have done so well.

And of course there are individuals who have helped us beyond anything we ever imagined. If I must single out one, it would have to be Rachel Carey-Harper, a Quaker and successful businesswoman who has provided us not only with considerable financial and case management support, but also with love and guidance and faith in us from the start. Rachel is the helper of the helpers. She is a guardian, a protector of those at risk, in need, or oppressed. She advocates for businesspersons to invest in organizations working with the poor. She contends that in doing so, as Scripture says, you will reap rich rewards, both spiritual and financial. Rachel's very generous donation, along with a sizable donation from the Cape Cod Council of Churches, enabled HNH to buy a seven-bedroom house. Four years ago we began with one home, housing five. Then we were able to house twenty-four formerly homeless men and women in three homes. Now I am pleased to report that in the fall of 2012 we purchased our second home, Eve's House, which will provide housing for ten to fourteen women. We're a young organization, only five years old, but we own two of our four houses. We are now providing supportive housing for thirty-six to forty women. Our goal is to own all our houses, which will make our organization completely self-sustaining. Our larger goal is to demonstrate to other communities that our model for providing education and housing for the homeless is both effective and affordable.

In summary, Alan, I want to express my gratitude to you and to everyone who has taken the time to love and help us. Through nothing less than miracles and angels in our midst, something very strange and mystical happened along the way. The seeds of love were planted, and they brought forth buds of kindness and good deeds. These buds came from everywhere. They sprouted in some who initially hated us, opposed us, even tried to hurt us. They sprouted up in those who felt powerless to make a difference and then became powerful leaders and makers of change. They sprang forth in our youth in the schools who wrote us letters, raised community awareness and money to help us succeed and expand. It came from the churches, synagogues, Quaker meetings, and from so many other places expected and unexpected.

How shall I finish here? It's like there was darkness and then the light of love came, which brought forth the way to lift up the downhearted. In the end, everyone has been blessed here. The helpers and those helped: all have been blessed, so very blessed. Now, the work is still there and there is so much more to be done. I just want to thank so many for so much that has been done already.

Billy, is there anything else you want to say?

Yes. I want to say that we are all brothers and sisters, fathers and mothers, sons and daughters. We are a family, and we are responsible for each other. Now, it's one thing to say we believe in this and another to really do it. I'm saying that we have allowed thousands of men, women, and children to suffer in poverty and homelessness right before our eyes. This is not good for them and certainly not good for us. We cannot really be happy and fulfilled with our lives while others are suffering around us. We must share our resources fairly with everyone. If this means that we have a little less so that others can have what they desperately need, then this is the way it should and must be.

Our lives are short no matter how you look at it. It is therefore so important for us to wake up and step up to our responsibilities to take care of those in need. It is our responsibility to take the time to go out and find the lost sheep and bring them safely home. Let us expect this of ourselves, our families, our loved ones, our communities. There's really nothing left for me to say, just love as much as you can as long as you can. This is what I'm doing and I'm having the time of my life.

CHAPTER 6

Some Concluding Thoughts

MY INITIAL TITLE FOR this book was *The Burden of the Blessing*. Although it should be clear by now that I love this work, it is a burden in significant ways. I did not choose this work. It fell down upon me, a calling from God, a burden for me to bear. I knew from the very moment I turned into the parking lot of the Salvation Army in 1993 that my life would never be the same. However, in this commitment, this work, this burden, I have become closer to God and found rich meaning in my life. Hence the title *Blessings of the Burden*.

And even though I'm very grateful, there are days when I feel like this blessing is more of a burden. This is especially true after someone I know dies, or when I realize I can't help someone desperately in need. I'm usually in my car, driving home, when the sadness and anger wells up inside me. Soon I'm having another very difficult conversation with God that goes something like this:

> God, I have done what you asked of me. I have loved and I have helped the homeless for many years now. I have done much more than my share. I've sacrificed so much for this: time with my family, my friends, my life. I've done my part. Let me go. Let me go. I don't want to hear another sad story, or learn about another death on the streets. Let me go. Let me have a normal life like everyone else. I'm obsessed with this

work. It's ruining my life. It's not right, let me go. Please, just let me go from this.

I ride on in silence, thinking, *It's too late. I've gone too far down this road. There is no turning back. There is no turning back. This is my burden to carry forever.* My sadness and anger end as I pull into my driveway and see my beautiful house, knowing that my beautiful family is inside. I start to cry again as I feel so fortunate. I take a few deep breaths, call it a day, and go into the house to unwind, spend a little time with my family, then go to sleep to be rested up for another day. The life I've chosen is difficult. It is a burden. But more than that, it is a blessing.

In the giving, we receive. In the sacrifice, we gain so much in return. In the loving, we are loved. In the helping, we are helped. In all of this work of loving and helping those most in need, we become closer to God and nothing is more important than this.

In finishing this book, I feel content that I have said what needed to be said. And in the bigger picture, I feel content in what I have accomplished in my work for the homeless. I have become an important and respected voice for them. I have helped to create and develop some important programs that have helped them. I have coordinated the help of dozens of churches and places of worship to help the homeless in a number of ways. I have helped hundreds of homeless men and women into housing. I have also developed some personal and effective relationships with key persons working on the issue of homelessness.

At the same time, I can't help but feel a bit unsatisfied. There is so much more that needs to be said and done by so many before any of us should feel comfortable that our homeless neighbors are getting enough love, support, and resources. At this time we are forced to pick and choose who will or will not get helped, who will or will not die. I wrote about this in one of many articles I have written for the *Cape Cod Times* (January 26, 2007):

Who Decides Who Lives, Who Dies

The other night I was trying to help a homeless man off the streets. He was intoxicated so I could not safely help him into a church for the night. I asked about helping him into a detox. His response to me seemed a bit rude at first, but as time passed, his words became more disturbing to me. He said, "I've been to detox. What's the point to come back to this? Never mind, I see you're the one who decides who lives and who dies." He then walked away. I never saw him again.

The words of this man continue to haunt me with the sad truth. He was right. What is the point of detox or rehab when someone who is unable to work because of mental illness or disability will eventually be released back onto the street? What is the point, and why wouldn't someone use alcohol or drugs to kill the pain of loneliness, fear, and despair?

And just how should someone look, sound, or behave after having come to believe through painful experience that he or she is no longer welcome in the community, no longer welcome to exist?

Perhaps this man was not speaking to me alone. Perhaps I am only the messenger. In truth, each of us decides who will live and who will die in our community. We cannot escape this action by being quiet, by staying on the sidelines as if we had no part in the sentencing to death of our brothers and sisters living and suffering on our streets.

As a community, how long will we pretend that we can't hear what they want, what they need? They need a place to live that is affordable, as only in a home can they become well and human again. They need some of us to watch over them as good neighbors. They need our love and kindness to help them out of the hell of homelessness and despair.

The questions here beg answers from each of us.

At times people say I'm being overly dramatic and too critical of the work being done by our human services and housing organizations. I respond to this by saying that I know they are doing the best they can with the limited resources at hand. However, local, state, and federal support remains sorely lacking, which results in the continued and unnecessary suffering and deaths on our streets. How is it that we always have enough funds for wars but never enough to help our citizens in greatest need? I cannot be at peace until we, as a community and as a nation, do all that we can to help the homeless. And for those who argue that we are already doing all we can, I could not more strongly disagree.

As communities and as a nation we have the ability to provide housing and supportive services to all those in need. What's missing is our willingness to do so. By our neglect alone we show prejudice against the poor, the mentally ill, the sick, people of color, the homeless. As a nation we are functioning on the belief that everyone is responsible for themselves, so we provide them with minimal support and resources. Privately we each pray there will be help for us if we fall into any of these categories of dire need. Subsequently, we live in fear, so we hoard and don't insist that our leaders provide for those in need. We are afraid to see the poor, the sick, the homeless, and we pray we don't become one of them.

Dear brothers and sisters, it is imperative that we begin to change our daily routines to include helping those most in need. As we do this, we will begin to find real peace, real happiness, real meaning, and real purpose in our lives. In the helping, we are helped. In the blessing, we are blessed. The burden is a blessing.

Our challenge is to break our addiction to fulfilling our own desires and instead give our attention to and share our resources with the less fortunate. This doesn't mean we need to give all of our time and resources away. It does mean making a commitment to include loving and helping those in need as a routine part of our lives. There are many opportunities in our communities for us to do extend ourselves to others less fortunate. As Billy says, "It's about waking up and stepping up to the plate of loving and helping others."

One more short story to speak further on this point: about forty years ago I tried to explain something I had learned in school to my grandmother. I told her that psychologists use the analogy that people who think positively and live productive lives see the glass of life as half full, while people who are negatively minded and unproductive see the same glass of life as half empty. My grandmother said that this theory didn't make any sense to her. I tried again to explain it. But again she said it didn't make any sense to her. So I asked what she thought made sense. Grandma went on to say, "The glass isn't half full and it certainly isn't half empty. Instead, the glass is overflowing."

I was intrigued by her answer and asked for more. She said, "Alan, God gives each of us more than what we need. This is what I mean that the glass is overflowing. Once you realize how blessed you have been, you want to spend the rest of your life sharing this wealth, this blessing of love with others." Although my grandmother died shortly after imparting this wisdom of love upon me, her words empowered me, transformed me forever.

My grandmother was right. I have seen this transformation in so many others who have discovered that their glasses are overflowing. This transformation happens so quickly and easily when we turn just a little bit of our lives over to helping those most in need. This is the blessing of the burden. In blessing, we are blessed.

Just as I began this book, I can now feel the presence of my friend Henry behind me. He is whispering, "Nice book. It will sell, and the money will help you to help the homeless. You wait and see." In my mind's eye, I can see Henry's beautiful face and something else. Is that you, God? Amen.

I awoke one morning
to the realization
I was a child of God

Ever since then
I knew who I was
and the purpose
for my life
all our lives:
We are here to love.

ACKNOWLEDGMENTS

A whole series of books could and should be written about those dedicated men and women who have done so much to help the homeless. Within the confines of this book I have only been able to single out a few of these angels among us, but I hope that mentioning them will encourage readers to realize that they have exceptional individuals and organizations in their own communities who can become more meaningfully involved in developing the ways to better help the homeless. Indeed, this is one of the key reasons why I have written this book. We can all do so much more, especially when we join hands.

The idea is for us to get involved — or more involved — with the needs of the homeless. We begin by looking for the holes in the system, learning about the lack of funds and resources. We then ask the human services and housing experts for ideas on how to make things better. Armed with this information, we then go to the people of faith, to the community members, businesspersons, organizations, and media in an outcry and plea for help to make things better for those most in need.

Dear friends, I encourage you to be courageous and to believe in yourselves and your community to do something amazing. As people of faith, we have the greatest force upon the earth, the power of love. It is ours. Let's use it.

In addition to the few persons I have already mentioned, I want to include a few more individuals who have been so importantly involved in my life and this work.

First and foremost, I am grateful to the woman I love, my wife Dawn. If it weren't for her, I would never have done any of this work, would not have written this book. Simply put, Dawn dragged me into the helping profession thirty-seven years ago. I was working for the highway department and she was working in a nursing home. I had no interest in or intention of getting into human services. However, Dawn had other plans for me. On Saturdays she would take me to the nursing home to visit some of her patients. At first I stayed in the car for many of the visits; in truth, I was afraid to go in.

Yet one day she convinced me of the importance of going in. Dawn held my hand and assured me that I would be okay. As I walked out of the nursing home, there were tears in my eyes. Although I could not have expressed it at the time, I had experienced God through the old, sick, and dying. As Mother Teresa once said, "In the face of the poor, the afflicted, the suffering, one sees the distressed disguise of God." I began working as an orderly, a job I held for four years, and have worked in human services ever since.

Although I seem to be the public face in our family for helping the homeless, Dawn has been a powerful advocate and resource for them. Over the years she has brought over twenty homeless men and women into our home. She has cooked for them, driven them places, encouraged and helped them. Some of them stayed with us for a few days, some for weeks, some for months, and a few for over a year.

Even as I write this Dawn is caring for an elderly man whom she invited to live with us. Several years ago he was told that he needed nursing home care and had to leave his home for medical safety reasons. Dawn went to visit him and felt moved to help him. At age eighty-seven, he has now lived with us for several years. We love him and will care for him until God takes him to heaven.

From the very beginning Dawn has continued to amaze me with her commitment to serving others in need. It continues to be Dawn who encourages and expects me to do all that I can to help those most in need. And though I continue to get most of the attention and credit, she continues to do so much, so quietly, behind the scenes. She amazes me, blesses me.

There are Dawns in every community who are doing so much, so quietly behind the scenes. Your job is to find them, as they are an important and dynamic source of support and resources to help others to become actively and meaningfully involved with the homeless.

In 2002, as I was struggling to get the churches more involved in helping the homeless, I met with Diane Casey Lee, executive director of the Cape Cod Council of Churches. Shortly into that conversation, I confessed that I felt lost, overwhelmed, and helpless to help the homeless as I felt called to do. Diane lifted me up, telling me, "Like a basketball team, we are going to do a full-court press." With her leadership and continued guidance, support, and resources, our program has continued to expand and improve its services for the homeless.

I also owe much gratitude to Jill Scalise, an amazing Christian who helps the homeless in so many ways. Jill has been a huge source of support and guidance for me over the years. Through the Cape Cod Council of Churches, Jill works with me to coordinate with over forty churches to shelter the homeless. In addition, Jill provides case management and help in finding permanent housing for the men and women under our care. This program has provided over 32,000 church shelter beds and helped over 600 men and women over the past several years. Jill is an amazing source of love, kindness, resources, and encouragement to those most in need.

In so many ways, Deacon Ralph Cox challenges my whole understanding of retirement. I have never met a ninety-year-old busier than Ralph. He is an amazing example of a man fully dedicated to serving those in need, and he has continued to be a huge inspiration and resource in our efforts to help the homeless on Cape Cod. Not only does he coordinate the Overnights program in seven churches, he does much of the driving and the volunteer work. If you have a job to get done, ask the deacons; they are an amazing source of love and resource.

To the hundreds of volunteers from over forty churches and places of worship on Cape Cod, I extend my deepest gratitude. I would have to write many books to adequately describe the love, the commitment, the help you have provided our overnight guests. At a time when they were abandoned, you welcomed them into your churches. When they were hungry, you fed them. When they were lonely, you comforted them. When they were without hope, you reminded them of God's love and plan for them. In these and in so many other ways you have ministered to those most in need. In this, you are all so very blessed indeed. I have been amazed and inspired by you.

I cannot overemphasize the importance of seeking out the help and resources of your local churches' mission and outreach committees, as making miracles happen is their mission. Some of these outreach workers will be very helpful and some of them, like Jill and Ralph, will be absolutely amazing.

Once again I extend great admiration and appreciation to Rick Presbrey, CEO of Housing Assistance Corporation, and his amazing staff, who have provided so many important services to so many households. Not only have they prevented homelessness from happening in many situations, they have addressed its victims in every possible way. For example, though criticized by many for many years, Rick fought hard to keep the NOAH Shelter open, as it was a lifesaving necessity for many who had fallen to the streets.

Over the years I have been inspired by Paul and Caroline Hebert. About twenty years ago, they formed a large sober house complex on Cape Cod which has provided love and support to many homeless men and women. I have become close friends with Paul and Caroline and have been blessed, inspired, and guided by them. It is so important for us to find the people, the living saints, like Paul and Caroline, who have the desire, the faith, and the ability to create the missing resources that a community needs to move forward in a more progressive way to help the homeless.

I have also been blessed to know Bruce and Caroline Smith, who added a soup kitchen and housing to their church. In addition to preaching the Word, they live it through their love and service. They had to jump through countless zoning hoops to get the food pantry up and running and they did so with great determination and faith. Whenever I drive by Calvary Baptist Church of Hyannis, Massachusetts, I remember that Bruce and Caroline are living saints as well.

Although I have already praised the Duffy Health Care Center, I must make special note of Judy Best-Lavigniac, who was the first director of the Duffy Center. When I began my work with the homeless around 1993, I was a small voice speaking out. Judy took me under her wing and sided with me on every issue regarding the needs of the homeless. Unlike most of the other heads of organizations, who played it safe, Judy was outspoken, demanding that our community better respond to the needs of the homeless on Cape Cod. After the bulldozing of the homeless camps, it was Judy herself who drove the Duffy van to the woods to pick them up each day to provide care for them and return them to the camp each night. Judy was an amazing ally, and largely responsible for jumpstarting our community toward love, kindness, and help for our homeless neighbors.

Similarly, I owe much gratitude to Claire Goyer, who filled Judy's position as executive director when she left the Duffy Health Care Center. Claire expanded Duffy much further in its scope and mission. Following her, Heidi Nelson, the current director, has become a very important voice and leader in our community.

In the same way, I am grateful for Cheryl Bartlett, who was the executive director of Community Action of Cape Cod & Islands at the time I started my work. Like Judy, Cheryl led the charge through her many presentations urging the town and county to take responsibility for the homeless. In significant ways Cheryl risked her reputation. And to those of you in other communities, other states, who want to make a real difference, it is imperative that you seek out significant leaders like Judy Best-Lavigniac and Cheryl Bartlett, who are willing to put it all on the line for those most in need. Other important persons who respect them will follow suit.

In addition, I owe much to town councilors Royden Richardson and Janice Barton. Each of them has spoken boldly and extensively on the importance of recognizing and responding to the needs of the homeless. Without the voices, the positions, and the influence of community leaders like

Roy and Janice, it is difficult to advocate for a controversial issue like homelessness. I doubt I would have gotten very far without their courage, commitment, and advocacy. They supported and protected me all along the way.

There are no words adequate to express my deep gratitude and love for my Quaker Friends Rachel, John, Gail, Kay, Jim, Pavia, Lynn, Barbara, Jill, and Peter. Their support of my work with the homeless has been tremendous and so very important to me. Our clerk, Rachel Carey Harper, has been my spiritual guide for years and was among those who encouraged me to finish this book. Rachel does not like being in the limelight, preferring to help in the background. I'm sure I have already written too much about her in this book for her liking, so I will simply say that she is a bright light, a blessing upon the earth.

Kay Brown has gone over every sentence of this book and helped me to make many corrections along the way. Without her guidance and help, I would have never finished this book.

I must include a very special thanks to retired Major Norma Higbee, who got my position authorized with the Salvation Army, so that I was able to help the homeless and to become a part of this amazing Christian organization which provides food, shelter, clothing, and God's love to those in need around the world. Likewise, I am very grateful for the support I have received from Majors Ralph and Donna Hansen, who replaced Major Higbee when she retired, and from the current commanding officers, Captains Cynthia Brown and Katherine Corno. It has been an honor to work for the Salvation Army. I also want to acknowledge the inspiring artwork of Rick Perez, a former resident of Homeless Not Hopeless. He blessed us with his presence, his love, and his artwork.

I must also express my tremendous gratitude to Gabriel Fackre, retired professor, theologian, minister, and author, who continued to ask about the progress I was making with this book. Whenever I would give some sort of explanation or excuse for not having worked on it for some time, he would remind me that it was God who wanted me to write this book and to get it out to the world. And whenever my response to this expressed any doubt, Gabriel would say, "God wants you to think big. You have shared how you were inspired by God to write this book, so give it its just due. This is God working through you. Now get it out to the world." Well, Gabe, it is out!

Finally, I am grateful to everyone, everywhere, who has ever extended a loving and helping hand to the poor, the sick, the homeless. You are God's light upon the world.

More about Homeless
Not Hopeless, Inc.

To give readers more information about Homeless Not Hopeless, Inc., I include here the organization's mission statement, followed by material adapted from promotional brochures.

Mission Statement

Educate and advocate for the needs of the homeless. Help the homeless get off the street by providing food and shelter. Help them with medical, psychological, and spiritual issues. Help them to connect with available resources. Urge those who are capable to find employment or volunteer time. Facilitate acquisition of financial assistance for residents. Teach goal setting, occupational, and life skills that will lead to independent living.

"We Offer a Hand Up, Not a Hand Out"

Homeless Not Hopeless, Inc. (HNH), is a nonprofit corporation founded in 2007 to offer a helping hand to those in need of short- and long-term help. HNH offers affordable, supportive housing, educational training, and other tools to help our homeless become productive members of society. Our organization is actively managed by men and women who were formerly homeless themselves. They are aware of the problems and issues the homeless face and are equipped to help.

We currently have four homes, two for women and two for men. We are now providing near forty beds for homeless men and women on Cape Cod. As one of our board members, Deacon Dick Murphy, says, "Our success is clearly a sign that God is behind us in this important endeavor, that of housing and loving the homeless."

Residents of each home pay community fees. This is in keeping with HNH's goal of helping them to become self-sufficient and eventually move back into their communities as productive members.

We support our residents in a variety of ways:

- providing clean, safe, and affordable housing
- helping each person to become independent
- creating a welcoming and inclusive community setting
- providing support, respect, and encouragement
- allowing each person time to heal from living on the street
- teaching life skills to help individuals into independent living
- teaching job skills that will make individuals more job-ready
- providing transportation to important appointments
- providing access to medical support and counseling
- encouraging work or volunteer activities

"We Are Not a Program, We are a Family": The Origin and Journey of Homeless Not Hopeless, Inc.

Shortly before his death in 2003, George Anderson was quoted by the press as saying, "I may be homeless, but I'm not hopeless." George felt the pain of his situation and that of others suffering on the streets. "I've been waiting three years for my Section 8 housing certificate. Like others, I may die waiting," he said. And he did. However, along with George's despair, there was hopefulness, which George said came from the loving arms of the people of faith who loved and welcomed the homeless into their churches at night.

Several years later, a small group of homeless and formerly homeless individuals met with Alan Burt, the coordinator of the Salvation Army Overnights of Hospitality program which had sheltered George Anderson. These individuals would become the cofounders of Homeless Not Hopeless, Inc., an organization formed by and for the homeless. Although George had passed, the organization took its name from his words. In this way, George and all the others who had died in homelessness would be remembered and honored.

The cofounders shared the opinion that the homeless were the most important missing part in addressing homelessness. The idea was as simple as it was unique: "The homeless, with a little assistance, have the ability to take care of themselves."

The essential plan of this small group was to create a nonprofit organization that would provide a community-based approach to housing and helping the homeless. Toward this end, Billy Bishop signed a lease on two houses in the village of Hyannis. In the early fall of 2007, a dozen men and women from the Overnights program moved into the two residences, named Elise House and Faith House. Many churches provided funds, furniture, and other support to help these houses get off the ground. It was a beautiful partnership between the homeless, the churches, and the community.

During the first year of operation, the residents themselves became very involved in helping the organization to better understand and develop its ability to love and assist the homeless as they entered the houses. This challenged the typical program model, where residents are subordinate to staff. Instead, these houses were about the residents helping each other, the houses, and the organization to evolve and expand. In a significant way, the residents were and continue to be co-creators of Homeless Not Hopeless, Inc.

Under the leadership of Billy Bishop, the success of the houses improved dramatically from 35% in the first year to 85% in the second, third, and fourth years of operation. In significant ways Billy has been and continues to be the heart of the program. His ability to understand what homelessness is and does to individuals, and his ability to lovingly and capably help them back to health and well-being is awe-inspiring.

The houses of HNH are much more than places for men and women to live. Just as Billy Bishop is deeply involved with the rehabilitation of residents suffering from addiction issues, house managers are very involved in the teaching of basic life skills which many of the residents have lost or never developed. These educational, rehabilitative, and therapeutic services are an integral part of the program and are implemented in a personalized and loving way, preserving the feeling for each resident that he or she is at home and not in a typical and impersonal program setting.

In its fifth year of operation, HNH has purchased another house. It is now able to provide housing with love to nearly forty residents. In addition, this purchase provides greater financial stability to the organization.

On behalf of the entire board of directors, we welcome and need your support of this unique, meaningful, and very necessary organization. Our story is featured in the video *A Miracle on Cape Cod.*

Homeless Not Hopeless is a 501(c) nonprofit corporation. We exist on donations from our friends.

Please send donations to
HOMELESS NOT HOPELESS, INC.
310 Ocean Street, Hyannis, MA 02601

Office: 508-957-2334   *Fax:* 508-957-2335
Billy Bishop — 508-292-0255
bbishop@homelessnothopeless.org

Please check out our website and view the video at
homelessnothopeless.org

Further Resources

A wealth of information on the causes and conditions of homelessness is available from sources such as the following:

Center on Budget and Policy Priorities
820 First Street NE, Suite 510
Washington, DC 20002
202-408-1080
www.cbpp.org

Economic Policy Institute
1333 H Street, Suite 300, East Tower
Washington, DC 20005
202-775-8810
www.epi.org

Families USA
1201 New York Avenue NW, Suite 1100
Washington, DC 20005
202-628-3030
www.familiesusa.org

HOMES FOR THE HOMELESS
50 Cooper Square, 4th Floor
New York, NY 10003
212-529-5252
www.hfhnyc.org

INSTITUTE FOR CHILDREN AND POVERTY
44 Cooper Square
New York, NY 10003
212-358-8086
www.icphusa.org

NATIONAL COALITION FOR THE HOMELESS
2201 P St NW
Washington, DC 20037
202.462.4822
www.nationalhomeless.org

NATIONAL LOW INCOME HOUSING COALITION
727 15th Street NW, 6th Floor
Washington, DC 20005
202-662-1530
www.nlihc.org

NATIONAL PRIORITIES PROJECT
243 King Street, Suite 109
Northampton, MA 01060
413-584-9556
www.nationalpriorities.org

TECHNICAL ASSISTANCE COLLABORATIVE
31 St. James Avenue
Boston, MA 02116
617-266-5657
www.tacinc.org

U.S. BUREAU OF THE CENSUS
Washington, DC 20233-0001
301-763-8576
Health Insurance: www.census.gov/hhes/www/hlthins.html
Poverty: www.census.gov/hhes/www/poverty.html

U.S. CONFERENCE OF MAYORS
1620 Eye Street NW, 4th Floor
Washington, DC 20006-4005
202-293-7330
www.usmayors.org

U.S. DEPARTMENT OF HOUSING
AND URBAN DEVELOPMENT
P.O. Box 23268
Washington, DC 20026-3268
800-245-2691
www.huduser.org

PICTURES OF HOMELESSNESS

"I'm no longer a man. I'm an animal looking for shelter for the night." (Photo by Alan Burt)

"I was near frozen to death, in a panic for survival." (Photo by Alan Burt)

"The shelter was full, so I walked down the railroad tracks to find my own kind of shelter." (Photo by Alan Burt)

Unknown man on street corner. (Drawing by Rick Perez)

Woman on the street. (Drawing by Rick Perez)

Janis gives Andy a big hug. (Drawing by Rick Perez)